THE Spicy DEHYDRATOR COOKBOOK

95 Incredible Recipes to *Turn Up the Heat* on Jerky, Hot Sauce, Fruit Leather and More

Michael Hultquist, Founder of Chili Pepper Madness

PAGE STREET
PUBLISHING CO.

PAGE STREET
PUBLISHING CO.

Copyright © 2017 Michael J. Hultquist

First published in 2017 by
Page Street Publishing Co.
27 Congress Street, Suite 105
Salem, MA 01970
www.pagestreetpublishing.com

All rights reserved. No part of this book may be reproduced or used, in any form or by any means, electronic or mechanical, without prior permission in writing from the publisher.

Distributed by Macmillan, sales in Canada by The Canadian Manda Group.

21 20 19 18 17   1 2 3 4 5

ISBN-13: 978-1-62414-502-5
ISBN-10: 1-62414-502-7

Library of Congress Control Number: 2017443528

Cover and book design by Page Street Publishing Co.
Photography by Patty Hultquist

Printed and bound in China

  As a member of 1% for the Planet, Page Street Publishing protects our planet by donating to nonprofits like The Trustees, which focuses on local land conservation. Learn more at onepercentfortheplanet.org.

DEDICATION

This book is dedicated to all the creative cooks in the world who found a passion for food and feel the need to keep on learning and exploring. We are kindred souls.

It is dedicated to all the bold and spicy food lovers who visit our blog at Chili Pepper Madness—www.chilipeppermadness.com. We couldn't do what we do without your support. Truly, all of your comments and support mean so much to me.

And finally, to my wife, partner and best friend, Patty.

You are amazing beyond compare. You inspire me, always.

Contents

Why I Started Dehydrating

Dehydrating Basics and Benefits

Homemade Seasoning Blends and Powders
Fruit, Vegetable and Sauce Leathers
Hot Sauces
Making Jerky
Homemade Soups and Stew Mixes
Camping, Hiking and Easy Meals
Snacks and Munchies
Drinks and Infusions
Practicals

Acknowledgments
About the Author
Index

Why I Started Dehydrating

My passion for dehydrating was born from my passion for chili peppers. I never had much of a palate growing up, but as I grew older, I quickly realized I was a total chilihead. I found that I loved spicy foods, the spicier the better, and this took me straight into the wild world of hot sauces and chili peppers. I would snatch up hot sauces by the armload, and I started buying peppers by the bagful from wherever I could find them.

I took to cooking not long after I married, and I found myself incorporating peppers and other spicy elements into just about everything I made. After a while, I decided to share this particular passion by starting a food blog called Chili Pepper Madness. On the blog, I explore cooking with chili peppers of all types, as well as growing and preserving these wonderful peppers.

We started a garden on the side of our first home, and now we have a good-sized pepper patch around back of our current home. The garden grew until we were growing a dozen or more pepper varieties each year. We grew so many that I found myself preserving them any way I could. I froze them whole, cooked them down, froze sauces and purees, pickled and jarred them and turned them into jellies and jams. Then I purchased my first dehydrator.

Dehydrating is an ideal method for food preservation, a practice that goes back to ancient history.

My first dehydrator was a small model, a Nesco, perfect for home use, which I still use. I began by cleaning and slicing peppers into rings, dehydrating them overnight and using them dried in a variety of ways. I still do. I greatly enjoy using the whole dried pods by rehydrating them into hot sauces, crushing them and placing them into a dedicated grinder for dashing over foods, and grinding them down into powders so I can make my own spice blends. And now I not only use chili peppers, but also other fruits, vegetables and herbs. It is just something I truly love to do.

It didn't take long for my creative brain to reach out and ask the question, "What else can I do with this wonderful machine?" I had just begun to brew my own beer with my wife, and I always hated tossing out the spent grains after soaking them. It felt like such a waste, so rather than toss them out, I dehydrated them and used them for baking. Problem solved!

Next I turned to making jerky with different cuts of meat, experimenting with marinades and homemade rubs. I became a bit obsessed. I tossed all sorts of items into the dehydrator just to see what would happen.

I upgraded to a larger dehydrator, the Excalibur, and ever since I've been dehydrating with an eye toward useful creativity as well as practical preservation. Some of my favorite things to do with my dehydrator include:

- Making my own powders and seasoning blends.
- Making jerky.
- Making fruit and sauce leathers.
- Dehydrating cooked meals, like risottos and curries.
- Saving my spent grains!
- Making infusions.
- Making homemade snacks.
- Prepping camping food ahead so we can eat well around the campfire.

If you take a peek at the table of contents, you'll notice it closely mirrors the list above. So, basically, I've taken all of my favorite things to do with a dehydrator and turned them into this very book. This book, for you, is my contribution to the huge world that awaits you once you purchase your first dehydrator.

Yes, in writing this book, I assume you already own a dehydrator and have used it a few times. Maybe you've read the manual. Maybe you even own a few other books, and you've experimented a little. Or maybe you've been using one for years and you're looking for new ways to enjoy it. My goal here is not to dwell on the basics of dehydrating, which can be found easily within the dehydrator manual, but to explore some creative ways to use your dehydrated foods and ingredients.

The thing is, dehydrating is a simple thing to do when you break it down. That's part of the reason I love it. I like things to be easy. Nothing in this book is going to be hard to do. In fact, it's fun. To me, it's all very COOL. I love it. I hope you do, too.

Enjoy.

Dehydrating Basics and Benefits

Dehydrated foods have been around a long time. Early people learned they could dry certain food staples in the sun to help sustain them through the harsh winters and periods of food scarcity, as well as through long journeys. Throughout history, dried foods have been a staple in exploration and essential to human survival.

We've come a long way from the old days of sun drying, to a point where the act of dehydrating food is more scientific and certainly safer. Dehydrators allow us to dry foods with regular, controlled heat as well as continued air circulation to carry away the moisture, making dehydration much more effective. Gone are the days of variable sun temperatures and hopes for a breezy day.

Many of us don't equate drying foods at home with the art of survival. It isn't exactly why I personally dehydrate, though if there were a sudden zombie apocalypse, you might be further prepared than most with your cache of dehydrated foods.

Still, the benefits are clear. Dehydrating is one of the best methods to preserve foods.

The Benefits of Dehydrated Foods

Healthier
There is no need to treat your foods with chemicals that go into other packaging methods. Glance through the ingredients on most packaged goods at your local grocer, and you'll see the long list of chemicals that ultimately go into your body. Dehydrated foods need none of that. Dried foods also retain a high degree of their nutritional value.

Long Lasting
Dehydrated foods last longer than other preserved foods. Most of the food you'll be dehydrating at home can last easily in a cupboard for 6 months or longer, though if you prepare it properly, it can last for years.

Less Energy
Storing dried foods requires only a cool, dark location in oxygen-free packaging. There is no need for electricity, which is required for freezing.

Low Weight
With the moisture removed, dried foods are very low weight and easy to carry. Compare this with canned foods, and you'll be saving yourself a great deal of weight as well as space. I couldn't imagine carrying 30 pounds (13.5 kg) of carrots that have been canned, but I can easily imagine carrying 30 pounds (13.5 kg) of carrots that have been dehydrated, which would weigh far less.

Storage Space
Dehydrated foods take up very little space. I have a spot in my pantry with a few boxes that contain my sealed, dried foods. Cans take up much more area, as do the frozen foods overflowing in my freezer.

Simplicity
Hands down, dehydrating foods is the easiest method of food preservation there is, easier than canning for sure! I can literally dry my foods overnight while I am sleeping to build a stock of foods.

Tips and Basic Information

Read the Manual
Be sure to read and follow the manual that comes with your dehydrator model. There are several different dehydrators on the market, and while each operates in a similar fashion, they do have their differences. The biggest difference I see between models is the temperature recommendations. They aren't very far off, but one model might suggest 125°F (52°C) for a certain food, while another will suggest 130°F (55°C) for the very same food. Be sure to refer to your manual if you have temperature questions.

Preheating
It is smart to preheat your dehydrator before using it. I turn mine on at least 15 minutes before using, while I prep the foods, so it can warm up. This will limit the ability for bacteria to go to work at lower temperatures as the dehydrator heats up.

Practice Good Sanitation
Clean your dehydrator regularly, as some residue can build up within. It is best to wear gloves when dehydrating, not only for cleanliness, but also so the dried food does not pick up any moisture from your fingers.

Use a Mandoline
It really is the best way to get even slices. You want everything to be evenly sliced so it all dehydrates as evenly as possible.

Purchase Dehydrator Sheets
Your dehydrator comes with mesh trays, which will work for much of the food you are dehydrating, but the mesh won't work for certain foods, like leathers, drying sauces or other cooked meals. You'll need dehydrator sheets for that, which will not allow food to drip through. There are many brands on the market, so consider them all, depending on your brand of dehydrator.

Drying Times Will Vary
Always follow the drying times suggested by your recipe, though those times can vary because of a number of factors, including the thickness of your food slices, amount you are drying, moisture levels in your home, sugar content of the food and more. The best way to know if your foods are completely dried is to check them manually, so if in doubt, keep drying.

You Can't Over Dehydrate
Speaking of, you really can't "over dry" your foods, so if you accidentally leave your foods in the dehydrator for too long, they are still most likely okay. Fruit leathers are an exception, as they can become overly brittle, though they are still good to eat if you over dry them. This is not an invitation to leave your foods in the dehydrator indefinitely, but don't worry about over drying. Your biggest concern is under drying, so be sure to continue drying as needed until 95% of the moisture in your food is removed.

95%
This bears repeating. Always be sure to dehydrate your food until 95% of the moisture is removed. So, cool the food slightly after dehydrating and test for dryness. If moisture remains, the food can spoil. Moisture will feel sticky, so if you notice this, keep on drying.

Use a Top Quality Dehydrator
You deserve the best! Besides, higher quality tools result in higher quality products. It is best not to skimp on a dehydrator.

Lemon Juice
Lemon juice is a must for dehydrating. Or you can use ascorbic acid. It prevents browning of foods during drying. It also works as an anti-bacterial agent.

Foods to Avoid Dehydrating
Certain foods should not be dehydrated at home, as they require special equipment to dehycrate safely, or they are too high in fat content. Milk and raw eggs require special commercial drying processes that cannot be done at home, so if you require these for a recipe, you'll need to purchase them from an outside resource. Foods extremely high in fat will not dehydrate properly, such as butter, cheese and avocados. They will turn rancid quickly. Be sure to refer to your dehydrator manual for more information on these foods.

To Cook or Not to Cook
Many foods can be dehydrated raw, but some foods require a bit of cooking before dehydrating, so be sure to refer to your dehydrator handbook or manual for proper preparation. You may need to blanch or steam certain foods to dehydrate them effectively.

Storing Dehydrated Food
Dehydrated food should feel completely "dried." They should not feel soft or sticky and should snap when you bend them, depending on the type of food being dried.

Properly dried foods can seriously be stored for YEARS. But, they need to be stored properly and in the optimal environment. You obviously need to keep moisture away from these foods, so be sure to pack them away in vacuum-sealed bags or canning jars so no oxygen or moisture can enter. It is ideal to double bag them and keep them away from light and heat sources. Cool, dry and dark areas are best for storing dehydrated items.

Homemade jerky, however, is not meant for long-term storage. You can properly seal it, airtight, and keep it for about a month in a cupboard or up to a year in the freezer, but anything longer is not considered safe.

There is no definitive expiration date for how long dehydrated foods will last, so use common sense, properly handle and seal the dried foods, and store them in optimal environments.

HOMEMADE SEASONING BLENDS AND POWDERS

When I first developed an interest in cooking, I actively sought out different seasoning blends to flavor my food. I began with pre-made packets that only required meat and vegetables in a pot, but quickly found a variety of blends that could turn any meal from bland to grand. I progressed to purchasing bulk individual seasonings, such as ancho powder, granulated garlic, dried basil and Mexican oregano. This allowed me to blend my own version of certain seasonings that I used to purchase pre-made at the store.

With my dehydrator, I am now able to grow my own foods for drying and grinding into powders. I can also pick up interesting ingredients from the grocery store or farmers market and use them in unique blends. I can make chili powders and blends that are difficult to find anywhere else, like superhot chili powders or mixtures that satisfy my own personal preferences.

Dehydrator-wielding chefs have been cooking with their own self-made powders and dusts for years. Now you can, too. The secret is out.

I've included a collection of recipes that I find personally useful. Many can be adapted to your tastes. The All-Purpose Veggie Seasoning (page 14) can include herbs and your own personal favorite variety. The same goes for the Veggie Stock Powder (page 15). The Chili Powder (page 23) can be applied to any type of pepper. Use these recipes as a starting point to create your own interesting seasonings and blends.

Storage

Most seasonings can be stored in airtight containers for years, but they do begin to lose their potency after a month or so, so best practice is to dehydrate small amounts at a time. For longer life with less flavor loss, use a vacuum sealer.

Note: When I call for a "dried" ingredient, you have two options: buy it dried from the store or you can dehydrate it yourself. It just depends on your preference and how much time you have.

All-Purpose Veggie Seasoning

This particular blend of powdered vegetables truly is "all-purpose." You can use it as a base for soups and stews, in place of a stock, as a flavor enhancer for many dishes and even as a simple seasoning to sprinkle over your finished foods. It can be customized to your own personal tastes, so feel free to include or omit vegetables and herbs as desired. Speaking of herbs, be sure to use lower temperatures when dehydrating them, and dehydrate them separately from the vegetables. Higher temperatures and a too-long drying time will rob them of their fresh flavor and quality.

Makes 2½ cups (306 g)

3 medium yellow potatoes, sliced into ¼-inch (6-mm) pieces

1 pound (450 g) carrots, peeled and chopped into ¼-inch (6-mm) pieces

2 jalapeño peppers, sliced into ¼-inch (6-mm) pieces

3 large red bell peppers, sliced into ¼-inch (6-mm) pieces

3 large green bell peppers, sliced into ¼-inch (6-mm) pieces

1 large white onion, sliced into ¼-inch (6-mm) pieces

3 medium tomatoes, sliced into ¼-inch (6-mm) pieces

1 fennel bulb, sliced into ¼-inch (6-mm) pieces

6 celery sticks, sliced into ¼-inch (6-mm) pieces

6 cloves garlic, sliced into ¼-inch (6-mm) pieces

1 tablespoon (2 g) dried oregano

1 tablespoon (2 g) dried basil

1 tablespoon (2 g) dried parsley

Bring a pot of lightly salted water to a boil. Add the potatoes and carrots and boil for 5 minutes, or until they are tender. Drain, and plunge the slices into ice water to stop them from cooking.

Spread the potatoes, carrots, jalapeño peppers, bell peppers, onion, tomatoes, fennel, celery and garlic evenly over your dehydrator trays. Since we are working with large amounts, you may need to dry these in batches.

Dry at 130°F (55°C) for 8 to 16 hours. Some ingredients will dry more quickly than others, like garlic, onion and carrot, so check them after about 8 hours. Remove the ingredients that are completely dried, and add them to a large bowl. Keep drying everything until all of it is dried completely, and add everything to the large bowl.

For the herbs, if you'd like to start with fresh ingredients and dry them yourself, remove the stems and dehydrate the leaves at 95°F (35°C) for about 4 to 8 hours, depending on your amounts and humidity. Do not over dry the herbs, as you can rob them of their fresh flavors. You'll only need enough for 1 tablespoon (2 g) each, so save the rest if you do a large batch. Add the oregano, basil and parsley to the bowl with the dried vegetables.

Next, add the vegetable mixture in small batches to a food processor and process to form a powder. Sift through a strainer into another bowl and keep processing until it is all in powder form. You may have some residual chunks left, which you can keep or break apart with a mortar and pestle.

Store the powder in airtight containers and use as a seasoning. You can also use this as an alternative to stock by adding 1 tablespoon (8 g) per 1 cup (240 ml) of water.

Veggie Stock Powder

This recipe differs from the All-Purpose Veggie Seasoning (page 14) in that all of the vegetables are cooked down, much like making a stock. Gone are the days of buying vegetable stock. You will always have your own blend on hand to use any time.

Makes 1 cup (123 g)

1 large white onion, chopped

3 medium carrots, peeled and chopped

1 large bell pepper, chopped, or jalapeños or serranos for a spicier version

2 stalks celery, chopped

4 cloves garlic

2 tablespoons (5 g) chopped fresh parsley

2 tablespoons (5 g) chopped fresh thyme

4 cups (950 ml) water

Add the onion, carrots, bell pepper, celery, garlic, parsley, thyme and water to a large pot and bring it to a quick boil. Reduce the heat to low and simmer until the vegetables are very tender and only 1 cup (240 ml) or so of water remains.

Cool and puree the mixture in a food processor until it is smooth. Spread the vegetable mixture over dehydrator sheets and dehydrate at 130°F (55°C) for 8 to 10 hours, or until it is completely dried through. You should end up with a crumbly mixture.

Transfer this to a grinder and process to form a powder. Or, use a mortar and pestle to grind it down by hand. Sift it through a fine sieve for the best consistency.

Store the powder in airtight containers, and use 1 tablespoon (8 g) per 1 cup (240 ml) of water to make instant vegetable stock.

Citrus Salt

Citrus salt is simple to make, but an essential ingredient in our kitchen and bar. I enjoy using it as a finisher for meals like grilled or sautéed fish fillets. My wife likes to use it for salting the rims of drink glasses. Not only is it a nice presentation, but also it enhances a cocktail with extra flavor.

Makes 1 cup (200 g)

1 cup (200 g) flaky sea salt
2 tablespoons (12 g) lime zest
2 tablespoons (12 g) lemon zest

In a bowl, mix the salt, lime zest and lemon zest by hand. This will release the oils from the zest. Spread it out evenly on a dehydrator sheet and dry for 4 hours at 135°F (57°C).

Remove the salt from the dehydrator, and store it in an airtight container for use any time.

Roasted Garlic-Chili Salt

Roasted garlic is much mellower than raw garlic. It is deep and rich in flavor, without the raw garlic bite. Roast, then dry your garlic and grind it up with spicy chili peppers and salt for a seasoning you can sprinkle onto anything savory. I keep mine in a pinch jar next to the stovetop for finishing steaks or pork chops.

Makes ½ cup (100 g)

1 head garlic

1 tablespoon (15 ml) olive oil

½ cup (100 g) flaky sea salt, plus a dash

2 to 3 serrano chili peppers

Slice off the top of the garlic head so some of the raw garlic is exposed. Drizzle the garlic with olive oil and a dash of sea salt, and wrap it in aluminum foil. Roast the garlic in an oven at 400°F (205°C) for about 40 minutes, or until the garlic is very soft. Cool, and then squeeze the garlic out of the skins.

Mash up the roasted garlic with a fork and spread over a dehydrator sheet.

Slice the serrano peppers into rings and set onto a separate dehydrator tray.

Dry at 125°F (52°C) for 8 to 10 hours, or until completely dried. The peppers may dry more quickly, so check after about 6 hours or so.

When everything is completely dried and brittle, add the roasted garlic and dried serrano peppers to a food processor. Process until mostly smooth. Add the salt and pulse until the mixture is blended.

Add to a sealable pinch jar and use as desired. This will last for months, but the potency will begin to diminish after about a month or so.

Creole Bacon Salt

Bacon salt enhances the flavor of many different foods. Dash it over potatoes, either mashed or baked, for an extra bacon blast. Add a touch of decadence to healthier choices like pureed cauliflower. I enjoy it over brunch-style poached or hardboiled eggs, or as a creative way to rim a Bloody Mary cocktail.

Makes 2 cups (400 g)

1 pound (450 g) bacon strips
3 tablespoons (23 g) Creole seasoning
1 cup (200 g) coarse sea salt

Rub the bacon strips with the Creole seasoning. Make sure as much of it sticks as possible. Space the bacon strips out evenly on a baking sheet. Bake them for 30 minutes at 170°F (77°C), or until they are cooked through.

Blot dry and place the strips in a single layer onto dehydrator trays. Dry at 160°F (71°C) for 24 hours, or until dried through. Blot dry and flip the bacon every 4 to 6 hours for more even dehydrating. The resulting bacon jerky should be dry and rigid.

Crumble the bacon into a food processor and add the salt. Process to form a coarse, salty consistency.

Remove and store in an airtight container in the refrigerator for use any time.

Tequila-Lime Sugar

Like coconut and rum, tequila and lime are a perfect pairing. Sprinkle this over chocolate desserts, like piping hot brownies, or stir a bit into a hot cocoa. It is a fun bar ingredient to flavor sour drinks as well.

Makes ½ cup (100 g)

½ cup (100 g) sugar
¼ cup (60 ml) tequila
1 tablespoon (15 ml) lime juice
Zest from 1 lime

In a mixing bowl, stir the sugar, tequila, lime juice and zest to form a slurry. Pour the mixture over a dehydrator sheet, and dehydrate at 130°F (55°C) for 8 to 10 hours, or until completely dried.

Transfer the mixture to an airtight, sealable storage container and keep in a cool, dark place.

Coconut-Rum Sugar

Coconut and rum together is a classic combination, and that applies to this sweet blend. Use this particular blend to sprinkle over the tops of cakes or other baked goods, or to subtly flavor tea or an alcoholic drink. You can make the coconut powder by drying coconut per your dehydrator's instructions, then processing it until a powder forms.

Makes ½ cup (100 g)

½ cup (100 g) sugar
¼ cup (35 g) dried coconut powder
¼ cup (60 ml) rum

In a mixing bowl, stir the sugar, coconut powder and rum to form a slurry. Pour the mixture over a dehydrator sheet, and dehydrate at 130°F (55°C) for 8 to 10 hours, or until completely dried.

Transfer the mixture to an airtight, sealable storage container and keep in a cool, dark place.

Herbed Bread Crumbs

I like to use my dehydrator as opposed to the oven or toaster to make bread crumbs because the dehydrator allows for lower heat and a more consistent end product. Keep these herbed bread crumbs on hand for easy breading, but also as a crunchy crumble over main dishes or vegetable courses. You can use any variety of herbs for this mixture.

Makes 2 cups (300 g)

¼ loaf challah bread, sliced, or about 4 large slices
1 teaspoon dried basil
1 teaspoon dried oregano
1 teaspoon dried thyme
1 teaspoon granulated garlic

Set the bread slices on a dehydrator tray, and dehydrate at 155°F (68°C) for 6 hours, or until the bread is very dry and brittle.

Break the dried bread apart by hand and add the pieces to a food processor along with the basil, oregano, thyme and garlic. Process to form fine bread crumbs.

Store in airtight containers.

Homemade Seasoning Blends and Powders

Shrimp Powder

Homemade shrimp powder is another all-purpose ingredient that can be used for a huge variety of foods. It is briny and adds a level of umami to your final dish that you'll get nowhere else. It is ideal for Mexican or Asian cuisines, but don't stop there. Consider it for soups, dressings, dips and sauces. It is best to use smaller shrimp when making shrimp powder. They will process into a powder more easily for you.

Makes 1½ cups (180 g)

1 pound (450 g) uncooked shrimp, peeled and deveined

Salt

Bring a pot of lightly salted water to a boil. Add the shrimp, and cook for 2 minutes, or until the shrimp are nicely pink. Drain and cool. Larger shrimp should be chopped for more even drying.

Spread the cooked shrimp out evenly onto dehydrator trays, and dry at 155°F (68°C) for 5 to 6 hours, or until the shrimp are completely dried through.

Grind the shrimp in a food processor or with a mortar and pestle until it forms a flaky powder. Store in an airtight container. Freeze for longer use.

Note: You can also use pre-cooked shrimp for this recipe.

Chili Powder

This is for all the chiliheads out there. You know who you are! This process actually applies to ANY type of chili pepper, though I personally enjoy it most for making my own superhot blends. Superhot chili peppers are peppers that top 1 million Scoville Heat Units, making them extremely hot compared to other peppers. If you would prefer a milder resulting blend, use your favorite peppers and follow the same instructions. I use these chili powders as a component for making my own spice blends.

Makes 1 cup (123 g)

4 pounds (1.75 kg) fresh chili peppers

Clean and dry your peppers. Slice off the stems and slice the peppers into rings about ¼ inch (6 mm) thick. Place them out on your dehydrator trays, and dehydrate at 125°F (52°C) for about 12 to 16 hours, or until they are dried through. Thinner-walled peppers will dehydrate faster than thicker-walled peppers, such as bell peppers.

Once dried, process the peppers in a food processor until a powder forms. Sift the powder through a thin sieve, and process any remaining pepper chunks until you have only powder. Store in an airtight container. Freeze for longer use.

Fruit Powder

Fruit powder is an excellent ingredient to keep on hand for flavoring various dishes, both sweet and savory. Sprinkle the powder over your cereal or oatmeal in the morning. Use it as part of a seasoning blend or barbecue rub. Swirl it into ice cream, whipped cream or other desserts. It works particularly well with baked goods, where you can add it straight to the batter or mix it with the frosting. Fruits with a higher sugar content will be naturally clumpier, but can still form a flaky powder.

Makes 1 cup (123 g)

2 pounds (900 g) dehydrated fruit

1 teaspoon arrowroot, optional

Make sure your dehydrated fruit is completely dried through, as more pliable fruits with higher sugar content will not form a powder as easily. Set the dried fruit in the freezer for a few hours, or overnight. This will make the fruit easier to powder.

In a food processor, process the fruit until a powder forms. Remove any remaining chunks, and process those separately until only powder remains. You may have some caking, depending on the sugar content, but this is normal. A teaspoon of arrowroot helps with consistency if you feel it is too clumpy.

Citrus Pork Rub

Dried citrus isn't something easily found in stores, which gives you another powerful reason to own a dehydrator. Citrus pairs perfectly with just about any cut of pork, so a citrus-centric rub is one you'll want to keep on hand if you're a pork lover. I enjoy this on smoked ribs, but it's also ideal for pork chops and slow-cooked pork shoulder.

Makes ½ cup (62 g)

½ dehydrated orange
½ dehydrated lime
4 dried garlic cloves
1 teaspoon dried sage
1 teaspoon paprika
1 teaspoon salt
½ teaspoon black pepper
½ teaspoon cumin

In a food processor, process the orange, lime and garlic cloves until a powder forms. Add the sage, paprika, salt, black pepper and cumin and pulse until the blend is combined.

Use the blend as a rub for ribs, pork chops and more. It's also great with chicken.

Homemade Seasoning Blends and Powders

FRUIT, VEGETABLE AND SAUCE LEATHERS

If you ever had a fruit roll up as a kid, you've had what is called "fruit leather." A leather is different from dried fruit in that the fruit, along with other ingredients, is processed to more of a liquid-like state, and then dried. The process works not only for fruits, but for many vegetables as well, along with combinations of fruits, vegetables and seasonings. You are limited only by your own creativity and personal tastes.

Fruit leathers make for excellent sweet snacks, particularly if your goal is to exclude all of the preservatives and chemicals you may find in store-bought products. Making them at home is simple and absolutely worth the drying time.

Lucky for you, you are not limited to fruit. You can also make leathers from savory sauces and hot sauces. It's an ideal way to preserve foods for later use.

I enjoy making different hot sauce leathers, which may or may not incorporate fruit, that can either be enjoyed as a quick, spicy snack or as something I can easily rehydrate as a component of another dish.

Another smart way of cooking and preserving is to create leathers from homemade savory or sweet sauces. These sauces no longer need to take up space in your refrigerator or freezer. Make leathers from leftover sauce that you want to keep for later, or make a big batch of your favorite sauce that can be easily rehydrated whenever the mood strikes.

A quick example might be your favorite pasta sauce that you've dehydrated to form a leather. Take it camping with you and rehydrate it with boiling water and cooked noodles to enjoy your favorite homemade pasta, or save yourself time during the week by rehydrating a sauce that took hours to make in very little time. The flavor is just as outstanding.

Leather-Making Tips

In most cases I process my ingredients to a smooth texture before dehydrating, but you can leave them chunkier if you'd like. Also, consider blending different ingredients separately, then swirling them or mixing them on the dehydrator sheets to make interesting color patterns and shapes.

When making fruit leather, I like to incorporate honey because it is a natural ingredient, though you can use other sweeteners, such as corn syrup. It not only adds sweetness, but also will ensure that your leathers do not turn out brittle or crumbly. The sugar content provides flexibility.

From my experience, it is smart to invest in leather sheets, or dehydrator sheets, for making leathers. You can use parchment paper, but the leathers sometimes stick to the paper, making it difficult to remove them or keep the desired shape. Some dehydrators come with leather sheets, so be sure to use them, but if your model does not, you'll need to invest in some.

Flipping the leathers partway through isn't totally necessary, but it will cut down on your drying time. If you don't flip the leather, it will still dry through eventually.

Be careful not to over dry your leathers, as they can become brittle and crumbly, especially around the edges.

For presentation purposes, particularly if you are giving them away as gifts, trim your leather edges with a knife or kitchen scissors to a shape that is more easily rolled.

Storing Your Leathers

For longer-term storage, roll your leathers in parchment paper or wax paper to prevent sticking. Store them in airtight containers in a cool, dark pantry, and they will easily last 6 months to a year.

Sriracha Leather

The question is not "Why would you make Sriracha leather?" Instead, it is "Why would you NOT make Sriracha leather?" Sriracha enthusiasts abound, and the sauce has gained immense popularity in recent years, with more and more brands creating their own versions of it. The version served in the United States consists of chili peppers, sugar, garlic, vinegar and salt. Turning it into a leather intensifies the flavor.

Makes 3 sauce leathers, rehydrated to 1 cup (240 ml) of sauce each, or 24 coins, rehydrated to 1 tablespoon (15 ml) each

3 cups (700 ml) of your favorite Sriracha

Spread the Sriracha over dehydrator leather trays or drying sheets to ¼-inch (6-mm) thickness each, 1 cup (240 ml) of sauce per sheet. I use a spoon to spread it out as evenly as possible. This will help it dehydrate more evenly.

As an alternative, use 1 tablespoon (15 ml) at a time and create small circles of Sriracha. They will dehydrate into easy-to-use, single serving "Sriracha Dots" or "Sriracha Coins," which are great for meal additions.

Dehydrate at 130°F (55°C) for 4 to 5 hours, or until the leather peels away from the tray easily. You might need to use a knife to get along the edges, as it will be tacky, but it should not stick too much.

Flip the hot sauce leather, and dehydrate for 2 hours, or until it is completely dry and there aren't any moist spots left.

Cool it down a bit, and then roll it up. You can enjoy your sriracha leather now, or wrap it in plastic wrap and store in a cool, dry place. It will keep for 6 months or longer.

Mango-Habanero Hot Sauce Leather

Mango and habanero are best buds when it comes to flavor combinations. This leather will bring you a blast of tropical love, and HEAT, so beware. If you'd like to tame some of that heat, core the habaneros fully before using. Just be sure to wear gloves when handling. This leather is an excellent snack for spicy food lovers, and also works nicely when tossed into soups or stews for additional tropical flavor.

Makes 3 leathers

5 habanero peppers, chopped

1 mango, peeled and chopped

1 white onion, chopped

4 garlic cloves, chopped

½ cup (120 ml) apple cider vinegar

¼ cup (60 ml) water

2 tablespoons (30 ml) honey

¼ teaspoon cumin

½ teaspoon allspice

1 teaspoon ginger powder

1 teaspoon mustard powder

1 teaspoon salt

Add the peppers, mango, onion, garlic cloves, vinegar, water, honey, cumin, allspice, ginger, mustard and salt to a food processor or blender, and process until smooth. It should only take 1 to 2 minutes. Pour your spicy mix into a large sauté pan, and turn the heat on high. Bring the sauce to a quick boil, then drop the temperature and let it simmer for 10 minutes.

Remove from the heat and let the hot sauce cool down.

Next, spread the hot sauce over a dehydrator leather tray or drying sheet to ¼-inch (6-mm) thickness. I use a spoon to spread it out as evenly as possible, 1 cup (240 ml) per sheet. This will help it dehydrate more evenly.

Dehydrate at 130°F (55°C) for 4 to 5 hours, or until the leather peels away from the tray easily. You might need to use a knife to get along the edges, as it will be tacky, but it should not stick too much.

Flip the hot sauce leather, and dehydrate for 2 hours, or until it is completely dry and there aren't any moist spots left.

Cool it down a bit, and then roll it up. You can enjoy your hot sauce leather now, or wrap it in plastic wrap and store in a cool, dry place. It will keep for 6 months or longer.

Papaya-Pineapple-Grapefruit Fruit Leather

Whenever I come across papaya at the store, I either want to turn it into a hot sauce or a fruit leather. It is such a vibrant fruit with a soft, almost butter-like texture. Its sweetness, combined with pineapple and the sour from the grapefruit, makes for a nice treat.

Makes 3 leathers

1 cup (150 g) chopped papaya
1 cup (150 g) chopped pineapple
1 cup (225 g) chopped grapefruit
3 tablespoons (45 ml) honey
1 tablespoon (15 ml) lemon juice
2 tablespoons (30 ml) water
Pinch of salt

In a pot, simmer the papaya, pineapple, grapefruit, honey, lemon juice, water and salt. Cook for about 10 minutes, or until the fruit starts to soften and break down. Cool the fruit mixture a bit, then add it to a food processor and process it until smooth. Spread the mixture over a dehydrator leather tray or drying sheet to ¼-inch (6-mm) thickness. I use a spoon to spread it out as evenly as possible, 1 cup (240 ml) per sheet. This will help it dehydrate more evenly.

Dehydrate at 130°F (65°C) for 6 to 8 hours, or until the leather peels away from the tray easily. You might need to use a knife to get along the edges, as it will be tacky, but it should not stick too much.

Flip the fruit leather, and dehydrate for 2 hours, or until it is completely dry and there aren't any moist spots left.

Cool it down a bit, and then roll it up. You can enjoy your fruit leather now, or wrap it in plastic wrap and store in a cool, dry place. It will keep for 6 months or longer.

Star Fruit-Kiwi-Pineapple Fruit Leather

Get yourself a tropical mix of fruit together to make a homemade sweet snack. This combination brings me back to the beach.

Makes 3 leathers

1 cup (150 g) chopped star fruit
1 cup (150 g) chopped kiwi
1 cup (150 g) chopped pineapple
3 tablespoons (45 ml) honey
1 tablespoon (15 ml) lemon juice
2 tablespoons (30 ml) water

In a pot, simmer the star fruit, kiwi, pineapple, honey, lemon juice and water. Cook for about 10 minutes, or until the fruit starts to soften and break down. Cool the fruit mixture a bit, then add it to a food processor and process it until smooth. Spread it over a dehydrator leather tray or drying sheet to ¼-inch (6-mm) thickness. I use a spoon to spread it out as evenly as possible, 1 cup (240 ml) per sheet. This will help it dehydrate more evenly.

Dehydrate at 130°F (55°C) for 6 to 8 hours, or until the leather peels away from the tray easily. You might need to use a knife to get along the edges, as it will be tacky, but it should not stick too much.

Flip the fruit leather, and dehydrate for 2 hours, or until it is completely dry and there aren't any moist spots left.

Cool it down a bit, and then roll it up. You can enjoy your fruit leather now, or wrap it in plastic wrap and store in a cool, dry place. It will keep for 6 months or longer.

Apple-Mango-Pear Fruit Leather

The apples and pears give this an almost applesauce-like consistency, but the mango adds a smooth texture. The resulting flavor is subtle, but not overly sweet, with the cinnamon playing in the background.

Makes 3 leathers

1 cup (150 g) chopped apple
1 cup (150 g) chopped mango
1 cup (150 g) chopped pear
3 tablespoons (45 ml) honey
1 tablespoon (15 ml) lemon juice
2 tablespoons (30 ml) water
½ teaspoon cinnamon

In a pot, simmer the apple, mango, pear, honey, lemon juice, water and cinnamon. Cook for about 10 minutes, or until the fruit starts to soften and break down. Cool the fruit mixture a bit, then add it to a food processor and process it until smooth. Spread it over a dehydrator leather tray or drying sheet to ¼-inch (6-mm) thickness. I use a spoon to spread it out as evenly as possible, 1 cup (240 ml) per sheet. This will help it dehydrate more evenly.

Dehydrate at 130°F (55°C) for 6 to 8 hours, or until the leather peels away from the tray easily. You might need to use a knife to get along the edges, as it will be tacky, but it should not stick too much.

Flip the fruit leather, and dehydrate for 2 hours, or until it is completely dry and there aren't any moist spots left.

Cool it down a bit, and then roll it up. You can enjoy your fruit leather now, or wrap it in plastic wrap and store in a cool, dry place. It will keep for 6 months or longer.

Apple-Honeydew-Kiwi Fruit Leather

The buttery consistency of honeydew melon makes it an excellent choice for a leather. It has a natural sweetness, like cantaloupe without the aftertaste, and it makes a perfect trio when combined with apple and kiwi. Don't forget the touch of mint. This is great for a natural snack.

Makes 3 leathers

1 cup (150 g) chopped apple

1 cup (150 g) chopped honeydew melon

1 cup (150 g) chopped kiwi

3 tablespoons (45 ml) honey

1 tablespoon (15 ml) lemon juice

2 tablespoons (30 ml) water

1 teaspoon chopped fresh mint

In a pot, simmer the apple, honeydew melon, kiwi, honey, lemon juice, water and mint. Cook for about 10 minutes, or until the fruit starts to soften and break down. Cool the fruit mixture a bit, then add it to a food processor and process it until smooth. Spread it over a dehydrator leather tray or drying sheet to ¼-inch (6-mm) thickness. I use a spoon to spread it out as evenly as possible, 1 cup (240 ml) per sheet. This will help it dehydrate more evenly.

Dehydrate at 130°F (55°C) for 6 to 8 hours, or until the leather peels away from the tray easily. You might need to use a knife to get along the edges, as it will be tacky, but it should not stick too much.

Flip the fruit leather, and dehydrate for 2 hours, or until it is completely dry and there aren't any moist spots left.

Cool it down a bit, and then roll it up. You can enjoy your fruit leather now, or wrap it in plastic wrap and store in a cool, dry place. It will keep for 6 months or longer.

Mango-Jalapeño-Pineapple Leather

You don't have to limit your fruit leathers to only fruit. Introduce a spicy element by including a chili pepper into the mix, a jalapeño pepper in this case, which delivers a familiar level of heat. Each bite delivers a combination of sweet and heat, which is something I've always loved. Tamp down the heat by coring the peppers first, or make it even spicier by using hotter peppers, like the serrano or even a habanero.

Makes 3 leathers

1½ cups (225 g) chopped mango
1½ cups (225 g) chopped pineapple
2 jalapeño peppers, diced
3 tablespoons (45 ml) honey
1 tablespoon (15 ml) lemon juice
2 tablespoons (30 ml) water

In a pot, simmer the mango, pineapple, jalapeño, honey, lemon juice and water. Cook for about 10 minutes, or until the fruit starts to soften and break down. Cool the fruit mixture a bit, then add it to a food processor and process it until smooth. Spread it over a dehydrator leather tray or drying sheet to ¼-inch (6-mm) thickness. I use a spoon to spread it out as evenly as possible, 1 cup (240 ml) per sheet. This will help it dehydrate more evenly.

Dehydrate at 130°F (55°C) for 6 to 8 hours, or until the leather peels away from the tray easily. You might need to use a knife to get along the edges, as it will be tacky, but it should not stick too much.

Flip the fruit leather, and dehydrate for 2 hours, or until it is completely dry and there aren't any moist spots left.

Cool it down a bit, and then roll it up. You can enjoy your fruit leather now, or wrap it in plastic wrap and store in a cool, dry place. It will keep for 6 months or longer.

Ghost Pepper-Pineapple-Pear Hot Sauce Leather

For those who like it truly hot, the ghost pepper, or bhut jolokia, is one of the hottest chili peppers around, reaching over 1 million Scoville Heat Units. That is 3 times hotter than a fiery habanero pepper, or more than 100 times hotter than a jalapeño. For those of us who love very spicy snacks, this leather is for you.

Makes 4 leathers

3 cups (450 g) chopped pear
1 cup (150 g) chopped pineapple
2 ghost peppers, chopped
¼ cup (60 ml) apple cider vinegar
1 teaspoon honey
1 tablespoon (2 g) dried basil
1 teaspoon mustard powder

Add the pear, pineapple, peppers, vinegar, honey, basil and mustard powder to a large pot, and bring the liquid to a quick boil. Turn down the heat and simmer for 20 minutes, until the entire mixture breaks down and softens.

Transfer the mixture to a food processor or blender and process until smooth. It should only take 1 to 2 minutes.

Spread the sauce over a dehydrator leather tray or drying sheets to ¼-inch (6-mm) thickness. I use a spoon to spread it out as evenly as possible, 1 cup (240 ml) per sheet. This will help it dehydrate more evenly.

Dehydrate at 130°F (55°C) for 4 to 5 hours, or until the leather peels away from the tray easily. You might need to use a knife to get along the edges, as it will be tacky, but it should not stick too much.

Flip the hot sauce leather, and dehydrate for 2 hours, if needed, until it is completely dry and there aren't any moist spots left.

Cool it down a bit, and then roll it up. You can enjoy your hot sauce leather now, or wrap it in plastic wrap and store in a cool, dry place. It will keep for 6 months or longer.

Watermelon-Orange-Mango Fruit Leather

This fruit leather is a fun treat, with distinctive watermelon, tart orange and sweet, smooth mango. If you have a hard time finding agave, you can substitute it with honey, though agave has a more neutral flavor, which is better for this particular fruit combination.

Makes 3 leathers

1 cup (150 g) chopped watermelon
1 cup (225 g) chopped orange
1 cup (150 g) chopped mango
3 tablespoons (45 ml) agave nectar
1 tablespoon (15 ml) lemon juice
2 tablespoons (30 ml) water
Pinch of salt

In a pot, simmer the watermelon, orange, mango, agave, lemon juice, water and salt. Cook for about 10 minutes, or until the fruit starts to soften and break down. Cool the fruit mixture a bit, then add it to a food processor and process it until smooth. Spread it over a dehydrator leather tray or drying sheet to ¼-inch (6-mm) thickness. I use a spoon to spread it out as evenly as possible, 1 cup (240 ml) per sheet. This will help it dehydrate more evenly.

Dehydrate at 130°F (55°C) for 6 to 8 hours, or until the leather peels away from the tray easily. You might need to use a knife to get along the edges, as it will be tacky, but it should not stick too much.

Flip the fruit leather, and dehydrate for 2 hours, or until it is completely dry and there aren't any moist spots left.

Cool it down a bit, and then roll it up. You can enjoy your fruit leather now, or wrap it in plastic wrap and store in a cool, dry place. It will keep for 6 months or longer.

Kiwi-Blueberry Leather

There are so many interesting fruit combinations you can play with when making fruit leathers. I often enjoy combining colors that are starkly different from one another. I will cook them down separately, and make fun designs and shapes. This recipe uses small dots of dark blueberry over the light kiwi.

Makes 3 leathers, or 1 very large leather

2½ cups (375 g) chopped kiwi
3 tablespoons (45 ml) honey, divided
1 tablespoon (15 ml) lemon juice, divided
2 tablespoons (30 ml) water, divided
½ cup (75 g) chopped blueberries

Add the kiwi, half of the honey, lemon juice and water to a pot and bring to a simmer. To another pot, add the blueberries, remaining honey, lemon juice and water. Bring to a simmer.

Cook them both for about 10 minutes, or until the fruit starts to soften and break down. Cool both the fruit mixtures down a bit.

In a food processor, blend the kiwi mixture until smooth. Spread it over a dehydrator leather tray or drying sheet to ¼-inch (6-mm) thickness. I use a spoon to spread it out as evenly as possible, 1 cup (240 ml) per sheet. This will help it dehydrate more evenly.

Rinse out the food processor, and then process the blueberry mixture until smooth. Spoon the blueberry mixture over the kiwi mixture, forming small circles in a random pattern. Feel free to draw other shapes, like a smiley face or something else fun. Experiment!

Dehydrate at 130°F (55°C) for 6 to 8 hours, or until the leather peels away from the tray easily. You might need to use a knife to get along the edges, as it will be tacky, but it should not stick too much.

Flip the fruit leather, and dehydrate for 2 hours, or until it is completely dry and there aren't any moist spots left.

Cool it down a bit, and then roll it up. You can enjoy your fruit leather now, or wrap it in plastic wrap and store in a cool, dry place. It will keep for 6 months or longer.

Salsa Verde Leather

Salsa verde, made primarily from tart tomatillos and spicy chili peppers, is a staple in Mexican cooking. This is a version I enjoy making at home. Dehydrating is an ideal way to preserve salsas so they last a long time, and you lose no flavor at all in the rehydrating process.

Makes 4 salsa leathers, rehydrated to 1 cup (240 ml) of salsa each

- 2 pounds (900 g) tomatillos, peeled, rinsed and chopped
- 4 jalapeño peppers, chopped
- 4 garlic cloves
- 1 medium white onion, chopped
- 3 tablespoons (8 g) chopped cilantro
- ¼ cup (60 ml) white wine vinegar
- Juice from 1 lime
- Salt to taste

In a large pot, simmer the tomatillos, peppers, garlic, onion, cilantro, vinegar, lime juice and salt for 20 minutes, or until the entire mixture breaks down and softens. Break it down with a wooden spoon as you go along.

Transfer the mixture to a food processor or blender, and process until smooth. At this point you should have about 4 cups (950 ml) of salsa.

Spread the salsa over a dehydrator leather tray or drying sheets to ¼-inch (6-mm) thickness, 1 cup (240 ml) of salsa per sheet. I use a spoon to spread it out as evenly as possible. This will help it dehydrate more evenly.

Dehydrate at 130°F (55°C) for 5 to 6 hours, or until the leather peels away from the tray easily. You might need to use a knife to get along the edges, as it will be tacky, but it should not stick too much.

Flip the hot sauce leather, and dehydrate for 2 hours, if needed, until it is completely dry and there aren't any moist spots left.

Cool it down a bit, and then roll it up. Wrap it in plastic wrap and store in a cool, dry place. It will keep for 6 months or longer.

To rehydrate, add 1 leather to 1 cup (240 ml) of boiling water and remove from heat. It will rehydrate completely in about 20 minutes.

Fruit, Vegetable and Sauce Leathers

Spicy Red Salsa Leather

You can easily preserve your salsas by transforming them into leathers in your dehydrator. This applies to your favorite homemade recipes, or to any store bought brand. Leathers last a long time and take up very little space. Bring some along on your next camping trip and rehydrate to enjoy your favorite salsa around the campfire.

Makes 4 salsa leathers, rehydrated to 1 cup (240 ml) of salsa each

2 pounds (900 g) tomatoes, chopped

1 medium white onion, chopped

2 serrano peppers, chopped

3 cloves garlic, chopped

¼ cup (10 g) chopped cilantro

¼ teaspoon cumin

Juice from half a lime

Salt and pepper to taste

In a large pot, simmer the tomatoes, onion, peppers, garlic, cilantro, cumin, lime juice, salt and pepper for 20 minutes, or until the entire mixture breaks down and softens. Break it down with a wooden spoon as you go along.

Transfer the mixture to a food processor or blender, and process until smooth. At this point you should have about 4 cups (950 ml) of salsa.

Spread the salsa over dehydrator leather trays or drying sheets to ¼-inch (6-mm) thickness, 1 cup (240 ml) of salsa per sheet. I use a spoon to spread it out as evenly as possible. This will help it dehydrate more evenly.

Dehydrate at 130°F (55°C) for 5 to 6 hours, or until the leather peels away from the tray easily. You might need to use a knife to get along the edges, as it will be tacky, but it should not stick too much.

Flip the salsa leather, and dehydrate for 2 hours, if needed, until it is completely dry and there aren't any moist spots left.

Cool it down a bit, and then roll or fold it up. Wrap it in plastic wrap and store in a cool, dry place. It will keep for 6 months or longer.

To rehydrate, add 1 leather to 1 cup (240 ml) of boiling water and remove from heat. It will rehydrate completely in about 20 minutes.

Strawberry BBQ Sauce Leather

This particular technique applies to preserving any similar type of sauce. Dehydrating sauces is a great way to keep them for later so they don't go to waste. Sometimes I enjoy making large batches of my sauces just so I can dehydrate part of it for later use. This particular BBQ sauce is a good mix of tangy and sweet. One of my favorites, it is perfect for grilled pork or chicken.

Makes 3 sauce leathers, rehydrated to 1 cup (240 ml) of sauce each

1 tablespoon (15 ml) olive oil

1 medium yellow onion, chopped

1 jalapeño, chopped

3 cloves garlic, chopped

1 pound (450 g) strawberries, stemmed and chopped

¼ cup (60 ml) tequila

3 large tomatoes, chopped, or 1 (15-ounce [425-g]) can

¼ cup (60 ml) apple cider vinegar

¼ cup (45 g) brown sugar

3 tablespoons (45 ml) honey

3 tablespoons (45 ml) Worcestershire sauce

1 tablespoon (14 ml) of your favorite hot sauce, plus more for serving

Salt and pepper to taste

Heat the olive oil in a medium sized pot. Add the onion and jalapeño, and cook for about 5 minutes, until they begin to soften up. Add the garlic and cook about a minute, stirring, until it is nice and fragrant. Add the strawberries and cook for 5 minutes, breaking them apart. Swirl in the tequila and cook down for 1 minute.

Add the tomatoes, vinegar, sugar, honey, Worcestershire sauce and hot sauce, and stir. Add salt and pepper to taste. Bring the mix to a quick boil, and then reduce the heat to low. Simmer for 20 minutes to combine the flavors. You can simmer longer if you'd like to let the flavors develop even further.

Cool the sauce, and then process it in a food processor until smooth.

Spread the sauce over dehydrator leather sheets, 1 cup (240 ml) per sheet.

Dehydrate at 130°F (55°C) for about 8 hours, or until the leather peels away from the tray easily. You might need to use a knife to get along the edges, as it will be tacky, but it should not stick too much.

Flip the sauce leather, and dehydrate for 2 hours, or until it is completely dry and there aren't any moist spots left.

Cool it down a bit, and then roll it up. Wrap it in plastic wrap and store in a cool, dry place. It will keep for 6 months or longer.

To rehydrate, add 1 sauce leather with 1½ cups (350 ml) of water and bring to a quick boil. Reduce the heat and let it simmer about 15 minutes, or until the sauce is completely rehydrated. You may need a bit more water to achieve your desired consistency, depending on whether you want a thicker or thinner sauce.

HOT SAUCES

I've been making hot sauces for years. It has been one of my favorite activities since I started a garden. In fact, hot sauces are a big part of why I started gardening in the first place. When I first became interested in spicy foods, I couldn't get enough hot sauce. I would snap them up from the grocery store by the armload until I discovered the burgeoning hot sauce world. I had no idea at the time that there were so many outstanding artisan hot sauces on the market.

Today, the popularity of hot sauces has exploded, in large part due to the growing popularity of chili peppers. Once people discovered the ghost pepper, they began to push boundaries in seeking out hotter and hotter foods.

It didn't take long for me to begin making my own hot sauces. Not only is it fun to do, but it will save you a bit of money as well, especially if you're a big consumer of the stuff like I am. Also, making them at home allows you to experiment and produce flavors you might never find anywhere else.

It was through similar experimentation that I discovered you can make hot sauce from dehydrated ingredients. I typically grow a big variety of peppers and other foods, like heirloom tomatoes, and dehydrate many of them. I simply can't use them all fresh, and dehydrating them is the ultimate way to preserve them. One winter, I found that I had run out of my favorite homemade hot sauce, and I thought I'd try rehydrating some of the peppers and tomatoes to whip up a batch. I used the same recipe otherwise. I wasn't sure if it would turn out the same, but you know what? Happily, it sure did! The hot sauce was just as delicious as if I had made it fresh. Now I make a lot of my hot sauces from completely dehydrated ingredients.

In fact, some sauces and hot sauces can be BETTER than sauces made from fresh peppers, because you can lightly toast them in a dry pan before rehydrating, which adds a touch of smokiness and complexity to your final sauce.

Tips for Making Hot Sauce

For best hot sauce results, it is wise to experiment. Try different ingredients. Play with different peppers, even a variety of peppers, and other foods as well. Experiment with vegetables, but don't limit yourself to just veggies. Fruits are a great way to sweeten up hot sauces and add new dimension. Try different herb combinations and seasoning blends to develop your final flavors.

But, don't be afraid to keep it simple. Some of my favorite hot sauces use only 5 or 6 ingredients.

Consider your vinegar. Most hot sauces include vinegar, and your choice of vinegar will impact the taste of your hot sauce. White vinegar is mild and will let your chosen ingredients shine. Apple cider vinegar is sweeter.

Toasting your peppers is optional, but I do recommend it. I encourage you to try making your hot sauce both ways, first without toasting the peppers and then with the toasted peppers. Do you notice a difference? I do. I always lightly toast the peppers in a pan before rehydrating them, though your sauce will still taste great if you do not toast them.

Storing Hot Sauce

Hot sauce can be stored in the fridge in sterilized bottles, though you can keep them longer if you process them in a water bath for 10 minutes or longer. The target level pH for shelf stable foods is below 4.6 pH, but should be lower for home cooks, around 4.0 or so, to account for errors.

Enjoy your hot sauce!

Garlic-Habanero Hot Sauce

This is an extremely versatile hot sauce with plenty of heat from the habanero peppers. It is more of a finishing sauce to dash onto grilled chicken or pork, drizzle onto a burger or spoon over a sandwich.

Makes 1½ cups (350 ml)

15 dried habanero peppers

1 tablespoon (8 g) dried chopped white onion

½ teaspoon dried chopped garlic

2 teaspoons (1 g) dried cilantro

½ teaspoon dried lemon peel

½ teaspoon salt

1 cup (240 ml) white vinegar

¼ cup (60 ml) water

First, be sure to use dried ingredients that are dehydrated to your specific dehydrator's instructions.

Heat a large pan over medium heat, and add the habanero peppers. Lightly toast them in the dry pan for about a minute, flipping them once about halfway through.

Add the habanero peppers, onion, garlic, cilantro, lemon peel, salt, vinegar and water to a pot. Give it a swirl. Let it sit, without any heat, for 1 hour. This will rehydrate the ingredients.

Bring the pot to a quick boil, then reduce the heat and simmer for 10 minutes. Keep an eye on it. If too much liquid escapes, add in a bit more water, about 1 tablespoon (15 ml) at a time, to your desired consistency. I like mine to be a bit thick, so it can stick to a spoon, but if you enjoy a thinner sauce, feel free to add in more water or vinegar.

Cool it down, and then pour it into a food processor or blender. Process until it is nice and smooth.

Pour into sterilized bottles and enjoy!

Quick Chili-Garlic Sauce

This is similar to the chili-garlic sauce you can purchase in the Asian section of the grocery store. Now you can make it at home quickly and easily with dehydrated ingredients. I use it as a base for a number of different dishes.

Makes 1 cup (240 ml)

¼ cup (30 g) dried Thai chili peppers
1 tablespoon (8 g) dried garlic
1 tablespoon (13 g) sugar
2 tablespoons (30 ml) white vinegar
½ cup (120 ml) water
Salt and pepper to taste

First, be sure to use dried ingredients that are dehydrated to your specific dehydrator's instructions.

Heat a large pan over medium heat and add the chili peppers. Lightly toast them in the dry pan for about a minute, flipping them once about halfway through.

Add the chili peppers, garlic, sugar, vinegar, water, salt and pepper to a pot. Give it a swirl. Let it sit, without any heat, for 1 hour. This will rehydrate the ingredients.

Bring the pot to a quick boil, and then reduce the heat to low and simmer for 10 minutes. Keep an eye on it. If too much liquid escapes, add in a bit more water, about 1 tablespoon (15 ml) at a time, to your desired consistency. This works better as a thick sauce, but feel free to add in a bit more water or vinegar to your preference.

Cool it down, and then pour it into a food processor or blender. Process until it is nice and smooth.

Pour into sterilized bottles and enjoy!

Haitian Creole Hot Sauce

Scotch bonnet peppers bring a fiery heat to this taste of the tropics. Feel free to experiment with the amount of lemon juice you include in the recipe, as the amount can change the level of tartness.

Makes 1½ cups (350 ml)

½ cup (60 g) dried scotch bonnet chili peppers

2 tablespoons (15 g) dried onion

1 teaspoon dried garlic

1 tablespoon (8 g) dried tomato paste

3 tablespoons (45 ml) apple cider vinegar

1½ cups (350 ml) water

Juice from half a lemon

Salt and pepper to taste

First, be sure to use dried ingredients that are dehydrated to your specific dehydrator's instructions.

Heat a large pan over medium heat, and add the scotch bonnet peppers. Lightly toast them in the dry pan for about a minute, flipping them once about halfway through.

Add the scotch bonnet peppers, onion, garlic, tomato paste, vinegar, water, lemon juice, salt and pepper to a pot. Give it a swirl. Let it sit, without any heat, for 1 hour. This will rehydrate the ingredients.

Bring the pot to a quick boil, and then reduce the heat to low and simmer for 10 minutes. Keep an eye on it. If too much liquid escapes, add in a bit more water, about 1 tablespoon (15 ml) at a time, to your desired consistency.

Cool it down, and then pour it into a food processor or blender. Process until it is nice and smooth.

Pour into sterilized bottles and enjoy!

Ragin' Cajun Ghost Pepper Hot Sauce

Unleash the heat of the ghost pepper, or bhut jolokia, which measures more than 1 million SHU in the Scoville Heat Unit scale. While it is certainly hot, you'll find a pleasurable balance of fruitiness, tomato and Cajun seasonings along with an excellent level of heat. This is for true chiliheads.

Makes 1½ cups (350 ml)

½ cup (60 g) dried ghost peppers (bhut jolokia)

2 tablespoons (15 g) dried onion

1 teaspoon dried garlic

¼ cup (30 g) dried tomatoes

1 tablespoon (8 g) Cajun seasoning blend

3 tablespoons (45 ml) red wine vinegar

1¼ cups (350 ml) water

Salt and pepper to taste

First, be sure to use dried ingredients that are dehydrated to your specific dehydrator's instructions.

Heat a large pan over medium heat, and add the ghost peppers. Lightly toast them in the dry pan for about a minute, flipping them once about halfway through.

Add the ghost peppers, onion, garlic, tomatoes, Cajun seasoning, vinegar, water, salt and pepper to a pot. Give it a swirl. Let it sit, without any heat, for 1 hour. This will rehydrate the ingredients.

Bring the pot to a quick boil, and then reduce the heat to low and simmer for 10 minutes. Keep an eye on it. If too much liquid escapes, add in a bit more water, about 1 tablespoon (15 ml) at a time, to your desired consistency.

Cool it down, and then pour it into a food processor or blender. Process until it is nice and smooth.

Pour into sterilized bottles and enjoy!

Superhot Hot Sauce

You can't really get any hotter than this type of hot sauce, unless you start using pepper extracts, which are somewhat bitter and not very pleasurable. Here we are using pure "superhot" peppers, which are the hottest chili peppers in the world. I grow my own peppers and dehydrate them for this sauce, though you can find fresh or dried pods online. If you thought the ghost pepper hot sauce was hot, wait until you try this one.

Makes 1½ cups (350 ml)

½ cup (60 g) dried superhot chili peppers, such as Carolina Reapers, 7-Pots or any of the Scorpion varieties

1 teaspoon dried garlic

½ cup (120 ml) white vinegar

1 cup (240 ml) water

First, be sure to use dried ingredients that are dehydrated to your specific dehydrator's instructions.

Heat a large pan over medium heat, and add the superhot peppers. Lightly toast them in the dry pan for about a minute, flipping them once about halfway through.

Add the superhot peppers, garlic, vinegar and water to a pot. Give it a swirl. Let it sit, without any heat, for 1 hour. This will rehydrate the ingredients.

Bring the pot to a quick boil, and then reduce the heat to low and simmer for 10 minutes. Keep an eye on it. If too much liquid escapes, add in a bit more water, about 1 tablespoon (15 ml) at a time, to your desired consistency.

Cool it down, and then pour it into a food processor or blender. Process until it is nice and smooth.

Pour into sterilized bottles and enjoy!

Caribbean Style Aji Hot Sauce

This is a fun little sauce with big tropical flavors. You may need to grow your own aji peppers for this one if you are unable to find any nearby. They aren't a pepper commonly found in grocery stores, though you can purchase dried pods online. Aji peppers have a wide heat range, depending on the variety. I used aji pineapple peppers for this recipe, though it will work with any aji. Try cayenne peppers for a local substitute.

Makes 1½ cups (350 ml)

½ cup (60 g) dried aji chili peppers

1 teaspoon dried roasted garlic

¼ cup (30 g) dried pineapple

1 tablespoon (8 g) dried coconut flakes

1 teaspoon dried ginger

½ cup (120 ml) apple cider vinegar

1 cup (240 ml) water

Salt and pepper to taste

First, be sure to use dried ingredients that are dehydrated to your specific dehydrator's instructions.

Heat a large pan over medium heat, and add the aji peppers. Lightly toast them in the dry pan for about a minute, flipping them once about halfway through.

Add the aji peppers, garlic, pineapple, coconut flakes, ginger, vinegar, water, salt and pepper to a pot. Give it a swirl. Let it sit, without any heat, for 1 hour. This will rehydrate the ingredients.

Bring the pot to a quick boil, and then reduce the heat to low and simmer for 10 minutes. Keep an eye on it. If too much liquid escapes, add in a bit more water, about 1 tablespoon (15 ml) at a time, to your desired consistency.

Cool it down, and then pour it into a food processor or blender. Process until it is nice and smooth.

Pour into sterilized bottles and enjoy!

Mild Poblano Sauce

Not every hot sauce needs to be scorching hot, or even hot at all. You can make savory sauces from milder peppers, such as the poblano pepper, which is one of my favorite peppers to cook with. Poblanos offer an earthy flavor that will liven up any dish.

Makes 2 cups (475 ml)

½ cup (60 g) dried poblano peppers
2 tablespoons (15 g) dried onion
1 teaspoon dried garlic
1 teaspoon dried Mexican oregano
½ teaspoon cumin
½ cup (120 ml) white vinegar
1 cup (240 ml) water
Juice from half a lime
Salt and pepper to taste

First, be sure to use dried ingredients that are dehydrated to your specific dehydrator's instructions.

Heat a large pan over medium heat, and add the poblano peppers. Lightly toast them in the dry pan for about a minute, flipping them once about halfway through.

Add the poblano peppers, onion, garlic, oregano, cumin, vinegar, water, lime juice, salt and pepper to a pot. Give it a swirl. Let it sit, without any heat, for 1 hour. This will rehydrate the ingredients.

Bring the pot to a quick boil, and then reduce the heat to low and simmer for 10 minutes. Keep an eye on it. If too much liquid escapes, add in a bit more water, about 1 tablespoon (15 ml) at a time, to your desired consistency.

Cool it down, and then pour it into a food processor or blender. Process until it is nice and smooth.

Pour into sterilized bottles and enjoy!

MAKING JERKY

Jerky making is a practice that dates back to ancient times and one of the most popular reasons to own a dehydrator. Removing moisture properly from meat limits biological activity, effectively preserving it for future consumption. It's easy to imagine early hunters leaving strips of meat to dry in the sun to keep for later use. Today, with refrigeration, there isn't quite the same need for dehydrating meat, though it still remains an effective method of preservation.

While sun drying meat is no longer considered safe by today's standards, a dehydrator allows you to apply a steady temperature and air flow in a controlled environment, which is important for proper food safety. The United States Department of Agriculture currently recommends making jerky only from meats that have been heated internally to 160°F (71°C), or 165°F (74°C) for poultry, so our recipes reflect this recommendation.

Of course it's important to follow good safety practices, but making jerky at home is easy and results in big flavors for snacks, energy for hiking and camping trips and easy meal additions for anytime consumption.

Let's break down the process for making jerky and dehydrating cooked meat.

Choose the best meats

Lean meats are best for long-term storage. Fat does not dry completely and will spoil more quickly. That said, my goal with jerky is for short-term storage and use, like for an upcoming hike or a weekend camping trip, or even for snacking, and these recipes reflect this.

You can also make jerky from ground meats, which is even easier because it requires no marinating.

A pound (450 g) of meat will yield you about 4 ounces (113 g) of jerky, so if you're concerned about weights, which is important for hiking, then plan accordingly.

Freeze it

Partially freeze the meat before slicing. This will help make slicing it much easier.

Slice it

Starting with a clean workspace and fresh meat, slice the meat into ¼-inch (6-mm) strips, or ½-inch (13-mm) strips for fish, that are 5 to 6 inches (13 to 15 cm) long. Slice against the grain for chewier jerky. Make them as even as possible so they dehydrate uniformly.

Marinate it

Marinate the strips overnight in your chosen marinade. Marinades bring in the flavor and help tenderize the meat. If you lack time, marinate at least 5 hours, but overnight is best for deeper flavor. Fish only needs a few hours to marinate. Alternatively, use a dry rub.

If you are making jerky from ground meats, you'll skip this step, but you will be adding in other ingredients and seasonings.

Cook it

Cook the meat either by steaming it or roasting it in the oven until the internal temperature reaches 160°F (71°C) for meat and 165°F (74°C) for poultry as read by a food thermometer. I prefer roasting, as it is easiest.

Dehydrate it

Finally, drain off the marinade, lay out the strips of meat in the dehydrator, and dehydrate at 160°F (71°C) for 6 to 8 hours, or until dried through. Times can vary a lot depending on the moisture content of the meat, the chosen meat, the temperatures in the house and various other factors, so check on the meat after 6 hours or so. You may also need to check the meat several times through the drying process to blot off any fats or liquids that rise up from the strips. Use a paper towel to dab it dry, and continue dehydrating. Some meats, such as bacon, take longer, so be sure to follow the recipes.

Storing Jerky and Dehydrated Cooked Meats

Make sure your jerky is dried completely. Store it in vacuum-sealed bags or airtight containers As mentioned, homemade meat jerky isn't made for long term storing, but it will keep for 1 month in a pantry, 6 months in the refrigerator and 1 year in the freezer. Salmon and other fish should be kept in the fridge or freezer and will last about half as long. If you'd like to make jerky for long-term storage, consider adding nitrites to the marinating stage.

Chipotle-Bourbon Beef Jerky

London broil is one of my go-to meats for jerky. It has a low fat content, which is ideal for making jerky, and it holds onto the flavors of your marinade quite nicely. This particular marinade is like a deep, savory barbecue sauce. It is nicely smoky from the chipotle peppers in adobo and bourbon, made slightly sweet with brown sugar and perfected with some of my favorite seasonings.

Makes ²/₃ pound (300 g) jerky

2 pounds (900 g) London broil
½ cup (120 ml) bourbon
½ cup (90 g) brown sugar
1 can chipotles in adobo sauce, pureed
2 tablespoons (30 ml) Worcestershire sauce
½ cup (120 ml) apple cider vinegar
2 tablespoons (15 g) onion powder
1 teaspoon ancho powder
1 teaspoon cayenne
1 teaspoon paprika
1 teaspoon dried oregano
1 teaspoon garlic powder
½ teaspoon cumin
½ teaspoon salt
½ teaspoon pepper

Wrap the London broil in plastic wrap and place into the freezer for about an hour to partially freeze. This will make slicing much easier.

Pull it out, set it onto a cutting board and slice it into ¼-inch (6-mm) strips. Thicker strips will take longer to dehydrate.

In a large mixing bowl, mix the bourbon, brown sugar, chipotles, Worcestershire sauce, vinegar, onion powder, ancho powder, cayenne, paprika, oregano, garlic powder, cumin, salt and pepper. Place the sliced beef strips into a large, sealable baggie, and pour the marinade over it. Seal it up, and massage the marinade into the beef with your hands. Get it in there good. Refrigerate for at least 5 hours, or overnight.

Drain the marinade and throw it away. Spread the beef strips out onto baking sheets and bake them for 10 minutes at 350°F (177°C).

Spread the beef strips out evenly onto your dehydrator trays.

Dry at 160°F (71°C) for 6 to 8 hours, or until dried through. Flip them after 4 hours. Blot them with a paper towel if you see any moisture oozing out. The resulting jerky should be pliable and should not snap when bent with your fingers.

Let them cool, and then wipe away any residual moisture.

After they've cooled, store them in airtight containers or enjoy them right away.

Sweet Habanero Chicken Jerky

Turn up the heat and sweet with habanero and honey. I like to make this chicken jerky for use in soups and stews. It rehydrates nicely and brings a lot of additional flavor. I do love it spicy.

Makes 1/3 pound (150 g) jerky

1 pound (450 g) chicken breast
10 habanero peppers, chopped
4 cloves garlic, chopped
½ cup (120 ml) white vinegar
¼ cup (60 ml) honey
½ cup (120 ml) water
1 teaspoon salt

Wrap the chicken in plastic wrap and place into the freezer for about 30 minutes to partially freeze. This will make slicing much easier.

Pull it out, set it onto a cutting board and slice it into ¼-inch (6-mm) strips. Thicker strips will take longer to dehydrate.

In a food processor, pulse the habanero peppers and garlic until they are finely chopped. Add the vinegar, honey, water and salt. Process until it is nice and smooth.

Pour the habanero mix into a large pan and bring it up to a quick boil. Turn down the heat and let it simmer for about 5 minutes. Remove from the heat and let it cool.

Add the chicken strips to a sealable baggie, and pour the marinade over them. Seal, and rub the marinade into the chicken with your fingers. Refrigerate it overnight.

Drain off the marinade and spread out the chicken strips on a baking sheet. Bake the chicken for 10 minutes at 360°F (182°C).

Blot the chicken dry and space the strips in a single layer onto your dehydrator trays. Dry at 160°F (71°C) for 6 to 8 hours, or until completely dried through. You may need to blot any fats from the dehydrating chicken part of the way through the process. The resulting jerky should be pliable and should crack, but not snap, when bent with your fingers.

Let them cool, and then wipe away any residual moisture.

After they've cooled, store them in airtight containers or enjoy them right away.

Mojo Pork Jerky

I first encountered "Cuban mojo" in a restaurant while on vacation in Florida, and I've been in love with it ever since. Cuban mojo is a sauce made from olive oil, garlic and bitter orange juice. If you can't find bitter orange in your area, use a combination of orange and lime juice instead. Pork is the perfect pairing for this sauce, so the mojo sauce makes a great marinade.

Makes $^2/_3$ pound (300 g) jerky

2 pounds (900 g) lean pork loin

6 cloves garlic, minced

1 serrano pepper, chopped

$^2/_3$ cup (160 ml) olive oil

1 tablespoon (2 g) dried oregano

1 teaspoon Chili Powder (page 23)

½ teaspoon cumin

1 teaspoon salt

1 teaspoon black pepper

Juice from 2 oranges

Juice from 2 limes

Wrap the pork loin in plastic wrap and place into the freezer for about an hour to partially freeze. This will make slicing much easier.

Pull it out, set it onto a cutting board and slice it into ¼-inch (6-mm) strips. Thicker strips will take longer to dehydrate.

In a mixing bowl, whisk together the garlic, serrano pepper, olive oil, oregano, chili powder, cumin, salt, black pepper, orange juice and lime juice to form the marinade.

Place the pork strips into a large, sealable baggie, and pour the marinade over them. Seal it up, and rub the marinade into the pork with fingers. Refrigerate it overnight.

Drain off the marinade and spread out the pork strips evenly onto baking sheets. Bake them for 10 minutes at 360°F (182°C).

Spread the strips in a single layer onto your dehydrator trays. Dry at 160°F (71°C) for 10 to 12 hours, or until completely dried through. At about the 5-hour mark, blot them dry with a paper towel, and flip them over to help keep an even dry. The resulting jerky should be pliable and should crack, but not snap, when bent with your fingers.

Let them cool, and then wipe away any residual moisture.

After they've cooled, store them in airtight containers or enjoy them right away.

Sriracha-Honey Bacon Jerky

Sriracha and honey are a power duo of flavor. They form a solid base for many sauces, which I enjoy using for chicken wings, base sauces and marinades. Bacon LOVES the combination of spicy and sweet, with just a touch of clove for additional character. Because of the fat content, bacon takes longer to dehydrate. It is best enjoyed right away.

Makes ⅓ pound (150 g) jerky

¼ cup (60 ml) Sriracha sauce

¼ cup (60 ml) honey

½ cup (90 g) brown sugar

1 teaspoon ground clove

1 teaspoon garlic powder

½ cup (120 ml) bourbon

1 pound (450 g) bacon, cut into ¼-inch (6-mm) slices

Whisk together the Sriracha sauce, honey, brown sugar, clove, garlic powder and bourbon in a bowl.

Place the bacon slices in a sealable baggie, and pour the marinade over them. Seal, and rub the marinade into the bacon. Refrigerate it overnight, or for at least 5 hours.

Drain off the marinade and toss it out. Space the bacon out evenly on a baking sheet. Bake the bacon for 30 minutes at 170°F (77°C).

Blot dry, and place the strips in a single layer onto dehydrator trays. Dry at 160°F (71°C) for 24 hours, or until dried through. Blot dry and flip the strips every 4 to 6 hours for more even dehydrating. The resulting bacon jerky should be dry and rigid.

Let the strips cool, and then wipe away any residual moisture.

After they've cooled, store them in airtight containers or enjoy them right away.

Mongolian Beef Jerky

Mongolian beef has a savory brown sauce made from hoisin sauce, roasted sesame oil, soy sauce, brown sugar and ginger. If you've ever had it at your local Chinese restaurant, you'll certainly want it in jerky form. All that flavor is intensified.

Makes ²/₃ pound (300 g) jerky

2 pounds (900 g) flank steak

2 tablespoons (30 ml) hoisin sauce

2 tablespoons (30 ml) roasted sesame oil

1 cup (240 ml) soy sauce

1 cup (240 ml) water

1 cup (180 g) brown sugar

2 tablespoons (15 g) fresh grated ginger

3 cloves garlic, minced

1 teaspoon black pepper

1 teaspoon salt

Wrap the flank steak in plastic wrap and place into the freezer for about an hour to partially freeze. This will make slicing much easier.

Pull it out, set it onto a cutting board and slice it into ¼-inch (6-mm) strips. Thicker strips will take longer to dehydrate.

In a mixing bowl, mix the hoisin sauce, sesame oil, soy sauce, water, brown sugar, ginger, garlic, pepper and salt to form the marinade. Place the sliced beef strips into a large, sealable baggie, and pour the marinade over it. Seal it up, and massage the marinade into the beef with your hands. Get it in there good. Refrigerate for at least 5 hours, or overnight.

Drain the marinade and throw it away. Spread the beef strips out onto baking sheets, and bake them for 10 minutes at 350°F (177°C).

Spread the beef strips out evenly onto your dehydrator trays. Dry at 160°F (71°C) for 6 to 8 hours, or until dried through. Flip them after 4 hours. Blot them with a paper towel if you see any moisture oozing out. The resulting jerky should be pliable and should not snap when bent with your fingers.

Let them cool, and then wipe away any residual moisture.

After they've cooled, store them in airtight containers or enjoy them right away.

Sweet Barbecue Bacon Jerky

This is one of my personal favorite barbecue sauces to make in the summer. I use it to slather over chicken, ribs and pork chops. It is outstanding on pork and, for me, it's a natural pairing with bacon, especially bacon jerky.

Makes ⅓ pound (150 g) jerky

½ cup (120 ml) balsamic vinegar

¼ cup (60 ml) apricot jam

1 tablespoon (15 ml) tomato paste

1 small onion, chopped

2 cloves garlic, minced

1 jalapeño pepper, chopped

2 teaspoons (10 ml) spicy stone-ground mustard

10 strawberries, chopped

1 teaspoon olive oil

2 teaspoons (10 ml) Worcestershire sauce

1 teaspoon brown sugar

Salt to taste

1 pound (454 g) bacon, cut into ¼-inch (6-mm) slices

Add the balsamic vinegar and apricot jam to a large saucepan, and simmer over medium-low heat until it has reduced to about ¼ cup (60 ml). Stir in the tomato paste, onion, garlic, jalapeño, mustard, strawberries, olive oil, Worcestershire sauce and brown sugar. Cook for about 10 minutes, stirring occasionally.

Transfer the mixture to a food processor, and process until smooth. Strain the sauce back into the saucepan, and season with salt to your personal taste. Heat through for 5 minutes, then remove from the heat and let it cool.

Place the bacon slices in a sealable baggie, and pour the sauce over them. Seal, and rub the sauce into the bacon. Refrigerate it overnight, or for at least 5 hours.

Drain off the sauce and toss it out. Space the bacon out evenly on a baking sheet. Bake the strips for 30 minutes at 170°F (77°C).

Blot dry, and place the strips in a single layer onto dehydrator trays. Dry at 160°F (71°C) for 24 hours, or until dried through. Blot dry and flip the strips every 4 to 6 hours for more even dehydrating. The resulting bacon jerky should be dry and rigid.

Let the strips cool, and then wipe away any residual moisture.

After they've cooled, store them in airtight containers or enjoy them right away.

Cajun Rubbed Chicken Jerky

Another way of making jerky is to work with a dry rub rather than a marinade. It's a time saver, as you don't waste the long hours waiting for the marinade to do its work. I cook with Cajun seasonings all the time on our food blog, and this particular blend gives a lot of POW to your chicken jerky.

Makes 1/3 pound (150 g) jerky

1 pound (450 g) chicken breast
1 teaspoon paprika
1 teaspoon cayenne powder
1 teaspoon garlic powder
1 teaspoon onion powder
1 teaspoon dried oregano
1 teaspoon dried basil
½ teaspoon thyme
½ teaspoon salt
½ teaspoon black pepper

Wrap the chicken in plastic wrap and place into the freezer for about 30 minutes to partially freeze. This will make slicing much easier.

Pull it out, set it onto a cutting board and slice it into ¼-inch (6-mm) strips. Thicker strips will take longer to dehydrate.

Mix the paprika, cayenne powder, garlic powder, onion powder, oregano, basil, thyme, salt and pepper together in a small mixing bowl and rub down each of the chicken strips with the blend. Press it into the chicken so it sticks. I like mine with a lot of seasoning.

Spread out the chicken strips on a baking sheet, and bake them for 10 minutes at 350°F (177°C).

Blot the chicken dry and space the strips in a single layer onto your dehydrator trays. Dry at 160°F (71°C) for 6 to 8 hours, or until completely dried through. You may need to blot any fats from the dehydrating chicken partway through the process. The resulting jerky should be pliable and should crack, but not snap, when bent with your fingers.

Let the strips cool, and then wipe away any residual moisture.

After they've cooled, store them in airtight containers or enjoy them right away.

Steakhouse Beef Jerky

Good steakhouses make their own steak sauces, and the quality shows. You can use this particular marinade recipe as a steak sauce if you process it and strain it. For now, we're using all the ingredients as a long marinade for that awesome steakhouse flavor.

Makes ⅔ pound (300 g) jerky

2 pounds (900 g) flank steak

2 tablespoons (30 ml) olive oil

1 large jalapeño pepper, chopped

1 medium white onion, chopped

3 cloves garlic, chopped

2 tablespoons tomato paste

½ cup (120 ml) Worcestershire sauce

½ cup (120 ml) red wine vinegar

¼ cup (45 g) brown sugar

3 tablespoons (45 ml) spicy brown mustard

1 teaspoon hot sauce

½ cup (120 ml) water

Salt and pepper to taste

Wrap the flank steak in plastic wrap and place into the freezer for about an hour to partially freeze. This will make slicing much easier.

Pull it out, set it onto a cutting board and slice it into ¼-inch (6-mm) strips. Thicker strips will take longer to dehydrate.

For the steak sauce marinade, heat the olive oil in a medium-sized pan and add the jalapeño and onion. Cook them down for about 5 minutes, then add the garlic and stir. Cook for another minute, until you can smell the garlic. Add the tomato paste and stir it in. Cook for about 5 minutes or so to darken.

Add the Worcestershire sauce, vinegar, brown sugar, mustard and hot sauce. Swirl. Reduce the heat and simmer for about 10 minutes to thicken it up. Remove from the heat and let cool.

Slip the sliced beef strips into a large, sealable baggie, and pour the marinade over it along with the water. Seal it up, and massage the marinade into the beef with your hands. Get it in there good. Refrigerate for at least 5 hours, or overnight.

Drain the marinade and throw it away. Spread the beef strips out onto baking sheets, and bake them for 10 minutes at 350°F (177°C).

Spread the beef strips out evenly onto your dehydrator trays.

Dry at 160°F (71°C) for 6 to 8 hours, or until dried through. Flip them after 4 hours. Blot them with a paper towel if you see any moisture oozing out. The resulting jerky should be pliable and should not snap when bent with your fingers.

Let the strips cool, and then wipe away any residual moisture.

After they've cooled, store them in airtight containers or enjoy them right away.

Ghost Pepper Beef Jerky

For those who love it HOT. Ghost peppers, or bhut jolokia peppers, held the title of "Hottest Chili Pepper in the World" for several years. It tops 1 million Scoville Heat Units, which measure chili pepper heat. A jalapeño, by contrast, averages around 5 thousand SHU. If you can take the heat, you'll notice that ghost peppers offer a pleasant, fruity flavor. I do love it hot!

Makes ⅔ pound (300 g) jerky

2 pounds (900 g) flank steak
1 tablespoon (15 ml) olive oil
6 ghost peppers, chopped
1 small onion, diced
2 small tomatoes, chopped
2 tablespoons (30 ml) red wine vinegar
1 teaspoon salt
¼ cup (60 ml) water, or more as needed

Wrap the flank steak in plastic wrap and place into the freezer for about an hour to partially freeze. This will make slicing much easier.

Pull it out, set it onto a cutting board and slice it into ¼-inch (6-mm) strips. Thicker strips will take longer to dehydrate.

For the marinade, heat the oil in a pan over medium heat and add the ghost peppers and onions. Be sure to turn on the exhaust fan or open a window, as the ghost peppers can fume up the air a bit. Cook them for a few minutes, and then add the tomatoes. Cook the mixture down for 10 minutes.

Add the vinegar, salt and water. Simmer the whole thing for about 15 minutes to allow the flavors to develop. Cool, and then process the marinade in a blender until smooth.

Place the sliced beef strips into a large, sealable baggie, and pour the marinade over it. If you need a bit more water to cover the strips, add in a little more as needed. Seal it up, and massage the marinade into the beef with your hands. Get it in there good. Refrigerate for at least 5 hours, or overnight.

Drain the marinade and throw it away. Spread the beef strips out onto baking sheets, and bake them for 10 minutes at 350°F (177°C).

Spread the beef strips out evenly onto your dehydrator trays.

Dry at 160°F (71°C) for 6 to 8 hours, or until dried through. Flip them after 4 hours. Blot them with a paper towel if you see any moisture oozing out. The resulting jerky should be pliable and should not snap when bent with your fingers.

Let the strips cool, and then wipe away any residual moisture.

After they've cooled, store them in airtight containers or enjoy them right away.

Chicken Fajita Jerky

Bring all the flavors of your favorite Tex-Mex to chicken jerky. Of course, you can go with a store-bought fajita-seasoning blend, but it is so much better when you mix it together on your own. This is my own fajita mix blend, but feel free to emphasize your preferred flavors by upping those ingredient ratios. Or, if you're like me, maybe add in a bit of ghost pepper powder to REALLY up the heat.

Makes 1/3 pound (150 g) jerky

1 pound (450 g) chicken breast
1 teaspoon cayenne powder
1 teaspoon paprika
1 teaspoon garlic powder
1 teaspoon onion powder
1 teaspoon dried oregano
1 teaspoon salt
½ teaspoon brown sugar
½ teaspoon cumin
¼ teaspoon ground black pepper

Wrap the chicken in plastic wrap and place into the freezer for about 30 minutes to partially freeze. This will make slicing much easier.

Pull it out, set it onto a cutting board and slice it into ¼-inch (6-mm) strips. Thicker strips will take longer to dehydrate.

Mix the cayenne powder, paprika, garlic powder, onion powder, oregano, salt, brown sugar, cumin and pepper together in a small mixing bowl and rub down each of the chicken strips with the blend. Press it into the chicken so it sticks. I like mine with a lot of seasoning.

Spread out the chicken strips on a baking sheet, and bake them for 10 minutes at 350°F (177°C).

Blot the chicken dry, and space the strips in a single layer onto your dehydrator trays. Dry at 160°F (71°C) for 6 to 8 hours, or until completely dried through. You may need to blot any fats from the dehydrating chicken partway through the process. The resulting jerky should be pliable and should crack, but not snap, when bent with your fingers.

Let the strips cool, and then wipe away any residual moisture.

After they've cooled, store them in airtight containers or enjoy them right away.

Turkey Taco Jerky

Turn your next "Taco Tuesday" into a taco jerky night. If you're camping, taco jerky rehydrates nicely, so you can easily enjoy your favorite tacos near the trails or around the campfire. I'm using ground turkey meat for this recipe because it is a leaner meat, and dehydrates better. You can make this with beef, but be sure to get the leanest product possible.

Makes 1/3 pound (150 g) jerky

1 pound (450 g) lean ground turkey

2 tablespoons (15 g) Chili Powder (page 23)

1 teaspoon cornstarch

1 teaspoon freshly ground cumin

1 teaspoon salt

1 teaspoon garlic powder

1 teaspoon paprika

1 teaspoon dried basil

Mix the turkey, chili powder, cornstarch, cumin, salt, garlic powder, paprika and basil together in a mixing bowl. Spread the mixture into ¼-inch (6-mm) thick strips on a large baking sheet. I like to use a jerky gun to make this easier, which allows you to make strips of various sizes.

Bake the strips for 10 minutes at 350°F (177°C).

Blot them dry, and space the strips in a single layer onto your dehydrator trays. Dry at 160°F (71°C) for 6 to 8 hours, or until completely dried through. You may need to blot any fats or moisture from the dehydrating meat partway through the process. The resulting jerky should be pliable, but should not snap when bent with your fingers.

Let the strips cool, and then wipe away any residual moisture.

After they've cooled, store them in airtight containers or enjoy them right away.

Buffalo Chicken Jerky

Buffalo sauce originated in Buffalo, New York, at the world famous Anchor Bar, where it was, and still is, served with chicken wings. It is primarily a mixture of hot sauce, melted butter and spices. It adds its characteristic heat and vinegary zing, and results in a tasty chicken jerky.

Makes ⅓ pound (150 g) jerky

1 pound (450 g) lean ground chicken
1 small onion, minced
1 jalapeño pepper, minced
2 cloves garlic, minced
¼ cup Buffalo sauce
¼ cup bread crumbs

Mix the chicken, onion, jalapeño, garlic, Buffalo sauce and bread crumbs together in a mixing bowl. Spread the mixture into ¼-inch (6-mm) thick strips on a large baking sheet. I like to use a jerky gun to make this easier, which allows you to make strips of various sizes.

Bake the strips for 10 minutes at 350°F (177°C).

Blot them dry, and space the strips in a single layer onto your dehydrator trays. Dry at 160°F (71°C) for 6 to 8 hours, or until completely dried through. You may need to blot any fats or moisture from the dehydrating meat partway through the process. The resulting jerky should be pliable but should not snap when bent with your fingers.

Let the strips cool, and then wipe away any residual moisture.

After they've cooled, store them in airtight containers or enjoy them right away.

Sesame Ginger Salmon Jerky

Salmon just might steal you away from beef if you're a diehard beef jerky lover. This particular recipe intensifies the flavors with a sesame-ginger marinade. You can eat jerky salmon just the way it is, or use it as an ingredient in other dishes, such as a salmon jerky crumble over pasta meals or swirled into a speedy brunch omelet.

Makes ½ pound (230 g) jerky

1½ pounds (675 g) salmon fillets
¼ cup (60 ml) sesame oil
2 tablespoons (30 ml) low sodium soy sauce
3 tablespoons (45 ml) rice vinegar
2 tablespoons (23 g) brown sugar
2 cloves garlic, minced
1 tablespoon (8 g) grated fresh ginger
1 tablespoon (10 g) sesame seeds
½ teaspoon ground black pepper

Wrap the salmon in plastic wrap and place into the freezer for about 30 minutes to partially freeze. This will make slicing much easier.

Pull it out, set it onto a cutting board and slice it into ½-inch (13-mm) strips. Thicker strips will take longer to dehydrate.

For the marinade, whisk together the sesame oil, soy sauce, vinegar, brown sugar, garlic, ginger, sesame seeds and pepper in a mixing bowl.

Place the sliced salmon strips into a large, sealable baggie, and pour the marinade over it. Seal it up, and massage the marinade gently into the salmon with your hands. Refrigerate for 4 hours.

Drain the marinade and throw it away. Spread the salmon strips out onto baking sheets, and bake them for 10 minutes at 350°F (177°C).

Blot the salmon dry, and space the strips in a single layer onto your dehydrator trays. Dry at 160°F (71°C) for 6 to 8 hours, or until completely dried through. You may need to blot any fats from the dehydrating chicken partway through the process. The resulting jerky should be pliable but should not snap when bent with your fingers.

Let the strips cool, and then wipe away any residual moisture.

Store them in airtight containers or enjoy them right away.

Sloppy Joes Jerky

When I was a kid, my mother made sloppy joes all the time, though they were out of a can. I've since learned, through a bit of experimentation, to make my own homemade version and got it just where I want it. Here it is in jerky form. Be sure to use lean ground beef, as fattier ground beef will be harder to dehydrate. You can make this with ground turkey or chicken as well.

Makes ⅓ pound (150 g) jerky

1 pound (450 g) lean ground beef

1 medium onion, minced

1 jalapeño pepper, minced

2 cloves garlic, minced

2 tablespoons (23 g) brown sugar

3 ounces (90 ml) tomato sauce

2 tablespoons (30 ml) spicy brown mustard

2 tablespoons (30 ml) Worcestershire sauce

2 teaspoons (5 g) cayenne powder

1 teaspoon paprika

2 tablespoons (30 ml) apple cider vinegar

Salt and pepper to taste

Mix the beef, onion, jalapeño, garlic, brown sugar, tomato sauce, mustard, Worcestershire sauce, cayenne powder, paprika, vinegar, salt and pepper together in a mixing bowl. Spread the mixture into ¼-inch (6-mm) thick strips on a large baking sheet. I like to use a jerky gun to make this easier, which allows you to make strips of various sizes.

Bake the strips for 10 minutes at 350°F (177°C).

Blot them dry, and space the strips in a single layer onto your dehydrator trays. Dry at 160°F (71°C) for 6 to 8 hours, or until completely dried through. You may need to blot any fats or moisture from the dehydrating meat partway through the process. The resulting jerky should be pliable but should not snap when bent with your fingers.

Let the strips cool, and then wipe away any residual moisture.

After they've cooled, store them in airtight containers or enjoy them right away.

Thai Basil Bacon Jerky

This is one of my wife's favorite bacon jerky recipes, based off of the popular Thai street food. Try it as part of the garnish for your next Bloody Mary.

Makes 1/3 pound (150 g) jerky

6 Thai peppers, chopped

4 garlic cloves, minced

¼ cup (10 g) chopped basil leaves

2 tablespoons (30 ml) fish sauce

¼ cup (60 ml) rice vinegar

¼ cup (60 ml) Simple Chili Oil (page 167)

1 teaspoon grated lime zest

1 pound (450 g) bacon, cut into ¼-inch (6-mm) slices

Add the Thai peppers, garlic, basil, fish sauce, rice vinegar, chili oil and lime zest together in a blender or food processor, and process until smooth.

Place the bacon slices in a sealable baggie, and pour the marinade over them. Seal, and rub the marinade into the bacon. Refrigerate it overnight, or for at least 5 hours.

Drain off the marinade and toss it out. Space the bacon out evenly on a baking sheet. Bake the strips for 30 minutes at 170°F (77°C).

Blot dry, and place the strips in a single layer onto dehydrator trays. Dry at 160°F (71°C) for 24 hours, or until dried through. Blot dry and flip every 4 to 6 hours for more even dehydrating. The resulting bacon jerky should be dry and rigid.

Let the strips cool, and then wipe away any residual moisture.

After they've cooled, store them in airtight containers or enjoy them right away.

Spicy Coffee-Maple Bacon Jerky

This bacon jerky is sweet with maple syrup and bold with French roast coffee. It is an ideal snack, but I enjoy crumbling it and cooking it into quiche or breakfast frittatas. Skip the chili flakes if you'd prefer a tamer version.

Makes 1/3 pound (150 g) jerky

½ cup (120 ml) bold French roast coffee, cooled

¼ cup (120 ml) pure maple syrup

1 teaspoon red chili flakes

1 pound (450 g) bacon, cut into ¼-inch (6-mm) slices

Whisk the coffee, maple syrup and red chili flakes together in a mixing bowl. Place the bacon slices in a sealable baggie, and pour the marinade over them. Seal, and rub the marinade into the bacon. Refrigerate it overnight, or for at least 5 hours.

Drain off the marinade and toss it out. Space the bacon strips out everly on a baking sheet. Bake them for 30 minutes at 170°F (77°C).

Blot dry and place the strips in a single layer onto dehydrator trays. Dry at 160°F (71°C) for 24 hours, or until dried through. Blot dry and flip every 4 to 6 hours for more even dehydrating. The resulting bacon jerky should be dry and rigid.

Let the strips cool, and then wipe away any residual moisture.

After they've cooled, store them in airtight containers or enjoy them right away.

HOMEMADE SOUPS AND STEW MIXES

Dehydrated foods make it simple and convenient to create unique and complex soups at home very quickly and with minimal effort. Who doesn't want to save time in the kitchen? In most cases, all you need to do is add your mix of dried ingredients to hot water, and let them rehydrate. In some cases, you'll only need to add an extra ingredient or two to bring them to life.

The flavors are the same as if you've just prepared the meal from scratch. You can use these soup and stew mix ingredients as simple starters to save time in the kitchen, process them with a food processor to make creamier soups, or add other ingredients like fresh chopped herbs, cheeses or freshly cooked meats or seafood to round out your dishes.

These recipes are similar in concept to some pre-made soup or stew mixes you might find in the store, though so much better as they are all completely homemade and contain no preservatives. They are also ideal for camping trips and make great gifts. Consider layering all of the ingredients in a jar, labeling it, and attaching printed instructions tied to a ribbon on how to reconstitute the dish. Who wouldn't love to receive the gift of hearty Cuban Yuca Soup (page 102) or tasty Winter Gazpacho (page 105)?

Jambalaya

Jambalaya is a Louisiana staple, particularly in and around New Orleans. It is hearty comfort food with plenty of rice, vegetables and a blend of spicy seasonings. This is more of a Creole version, which includes tomatoes. We've included dried shrimp with ours, though you can easily include chicken jerky if you're at the campsite. If you're at home, you may want to add freshly cooked chicken or andouille sausage.

Makes 2 to 3 servings

¼ cup (30 g) dried chopped onion

¼ cup (30 g) dried chopped bell pepper

2 dried roasted jalapeño peppers

2 tablespoons (15 g) dried chopped celery

1 tablespoon (8 g) dried chopped garlic

2 cups (245 g) dried chopped tomato

1 teaspoon dried oregano

1 teaspoon dried basil

½ cup (125 g) tomato sauce leather

1 cup (190 g) dried cooked rice

½ cup (62 g) dried chopped shrimp

2 teaspoons (5 g) Cajun seasoning blend

3 cups (700 ml) chicken or vegetable stock

Salt and pepper to taste

First, be sure to use dried ingredients that are dehydrated to your specific dehydrator's instructions.

Add the onion, bell pepper, jalapeño peppers, celery, garlic, tomato, oregano, basil, tomato sauce leather, rice, shrimp, Cajun seasoning, vegetable stock, salt and pepper to a large pot. Stir it up to incorporate, and bring it to a quick boil. Remove from the heat, and cover for 30 to 60 minutes to allow the ingredients to rehydrate.

Fluff the jambalaya with a fork and turn the burner back on to reheat, for about 5 minutes, stirring. You can add more liquid at this point if you'd like, to your own personal preference.

Caldo de Camaron (Mexican Shrimp Soup)

You'll enjoy this easy-to-make soup with zesty Mexican flavors and plenty of shrimp. You can use dried shrimp as I have done for this recipe, or add freshly cooked shrimp if you're cooking at home. The recipe also works well with cooked crab, scallops, langoustines or lobster.

Makes 2 servings

½ cup (62 g) dried chopped potato

2 tablespoons (15 g) dried chopped carrot

2 tablespoons (15 g) dried chopped onion

1 teaspoon dried chopped garlic

½ cup (62 g) dried chopped shrimp

1 tablespoon (8 g) guajillo chili powder

1 teaspoon dried cilantro

½ teaspoon dried lime zest

2 tablespoons (15 g) Veggie Stock Powder (page 15)

2 cups (475 ml) water

Salt and pepper to taste

First, be sure to use dried ingredients that are dehydrated to your specific dehydrator's instructions.

Add the potato, carrot, onion, garlic, shrimp, chili powder, cilantro, lime zest, veggie stock powder, water, salt and pepper to a large pot. Stir it up to incorporate, and bring it to a quick boil. Remove from the heat, and cover for 30 to 60 minutes to allow the ingredients to rehydrate.

Turn the burner back on to reheat, for about 5 minutes, stirring, and then serve it up.

Spicy Chicken Pozole

Pozole is a traditional Mexican soup with a great deal of history. It is prepared with hominy, which is made from corn, but not beans. You'll find different variations with many ingredient options that you can easily mix and match to your own tastes. This version includes chicken jerky, though you could also include dried shrimp. This dish is perfect for rehydrating at a campsite. If you're making this at home, top it with a bit of sliced avocado.

Makes 3 to 4 servings

⅓ cup (50 g) chicken jerky

8 cups (2 L) boiling water, divided

1 cup (123 g) dried cooked hominy

1 tablespoon (8 g) dried onion

1 tablespoon (8 g) dried jalapeño pepper

1 tablespoon (8 g) dried poblano pepper

1 tablespoon (8 g) dried bell pepper

1 teaspoon dried garlic

2 teaspoons (5 g) Chili Powder (page 23)

1 bay leaf

1 teaspoon dried thyme

2 teaspoons (5 g) cumin

¼ cup (62 g) tomato paste leather

1 teaspoon lime zest

Salt and pepper to taste

Sliced avocado and cilantro, for serving

First, be sure to use dried ingredients that are dehydrated to your specific dehydrator's instructions.

Add the chicken jerky to a large pot, and add 2 cups (475 ml) of boiling water. Let it sit for about 30 minutes to allow the chicken to rehydrate.

Add the hominy, onion, jalapeño pepper, poblano pepper, bell pepper, garlic, chili powder, bay leaf, thyme, cumin, tomato paste leather, lime zest, salt, pepper and the remaining 4 to 6 cups (950 to 1,440 ml) of water, depending on how brothy you'd like the soup, and on how many you're serving. Bring it to a quick boil, then remove from the heat and cover for 30 to 60 minutes to allow the ingredients to rehydrate. You can simmer for longer to let the flavors develop a bit more if you'd like.

Turn the burner back on to reheat, for about 5 minutes, stirring. Serve it with sliced or diced avocado and cilantro.

Cuban Yuca Soup

Yuca is popular mostly in the tropical regions of the world, where it is a staple carbohydrate. It is a root vegetable with a thick, coarse brown skin and a hard consistency. It needs to be cooked before dehydrating. While not strong on flavor on its own, it easily absorbs and highlights the flavors you choose to add to it. This recipe calls for milk powder, which should not be made in a home dehydrator. It needs to be purchased from a store. Or, use ½ cup (120 ml) of milk instead if you're making this at home.

Makes 3 to 4 servings

4 cups (950 ml) water

2 cups (245 g) dried yuca

1 cup (123 g) dried leeks

2 tablespoons (15 g) dried onion

2 tablespoons (15 g) Veggie Stock Powder (page 15)

2 tablespoons (15 g) milk powder

1 tablespoon (8 g) Chili Powder (page 23)

½ tablespoon (3 g) allspice

1 teaspoon salt

1 teaspoon black pepper

Fresh chopped parsley and lime, for serving

First, be sure to use dried ingredients that are dehydrated to your specific dehydrator's instructions.

Add the water, yuca, leeks, onion, veggie stock powder, milk powder, chili powder, allspice, salt and pepper to a large pot. Stir it up to incorporate, and bring to a quick boil. Remove from the heat, and cover for 30 to 60 minutes to allow the ingredients to rehydrate.

Transfer it all to a blender or food processor, and process until smooth and creamy. It should be fairly thick at this point.

Pour the soup back into the pot, and reheat it on medium-low heat for about 5 minutes, stirring.

Serve with fresh chopped parsley and a few squeezes of lime juice.

Apple-Butternut Squash Soup

The combination of sweet apple and creamy butternut squash is always a popular one. I enjoy adding a variety of dried chili peppers to the mix. Bell peppers are a good choice, but if you're in the mood for something a bit spicier, add in a dried jalapeño pepper or even a serrano pepper.

Makes 3 to 4 servings

6 cups (1.5 L) water

1 cup (123 g) dried butternut squash puree

1½ cups (184 g) dried chili pepper, any variety

¼ cup (30 g) dried green apple

1 tablespoon (8 g) dried onion

1 tablespoon (8 g) dried celery

1 teaspoon dried garlic

1 tablespoon (8 g) Chili Powder (page 23)

1 teaspoon dried rosemary

1 teaspoon dried basil

1 teaspoon Veggie Stock Powder (page 15)

Salt and pepper to taste

First, be sure to use dried ingredients that are dehydrated to your specific dehydrator's instructions.

Add the water, butternut squash, chili pepper, apple, onion, celery, garlic, chili powder, rosemary, basil, veggie stock powder, salt and pepper to a large pot. Stir it up to incorporate, and bring it to a quick boil. Remove from the heat, and cover for 30 to 60 minutes to allow the ingredients to rehydrate.

Transfer it all to a blender or food processor, and process until it's almost smooth, but still just a bit chunky. It should be fairly thick at this point.

Pour the soup back into the pot, and reheat it on medium-low heat for about 5 minutes, stirring.

Winter Gazpacho

We enjoy gazpacho made fresh from our garden vegetables each summer and fall, and now our dehydrator allows us to enjoy it in winter as well. All you need for this are your dehydrated vegetables, water, Worcestershire sauce and red wine vinegar. Delicious.

Makes 3 to 4 servings

1 cup (123 g) dried tomatoes

½ cup (62 g) dried mixed chili peppers

2 tablespoons (15 g) dried onion

1 tablespoon (8 g) dried carrot

1 teaspoon dried garlic

1 teaspoon dried basil

1 teaspoon dried parsley

1 teaspoon dried lemon zest

¼ cup (63 g) tomato sauce leather

1 dried Sriracha "dot" (page 29)

1 teaspoon Veggie Stock Powder (page 15)

5 to 6 cups (1 to 1.5 L) water

¼ cup (60 ml) red wine vinegar

2 tablespoons (30 ml) Worcestershire sauce

First, be sure to use dried ingredients that are dehydrated to your specific dehydrator's instructions.

Add the tomatoes, chili peppers, onion, carrot, garlic, basil, parsley, lemon zest, tomato sauce leather, Sriracha dot, veggie stock powder and water to a large pot. Stir it up to incorporate, and bring it to a quick boil. Remove from the heat, and cover for 30 to 60 minutes to allow the ingredients to rehydrate.

Stir in the red wine vinegar and Worcestershire sauce, and allow it to cool.

Transfer it all to a blender or food processor, and process until smooth. You can add more water if you'd like to achieve your preferred consistency.

Homemade Soups and Stew Mixes

Spicy Black Bean Soup

Black beans are my go-to for many soups and stews. They're popular in Mexican, Cuban and South American cuisines though, in my opinion, they are great with any cuisine. Beans rehydrate easily, and are an ideal match for the spicy peppers in this recipe.

Makes 3 to 4 servings

1½ cups (306 g) dried cooked black beans

½ cup (62 g) dried crumbled bell peppers

1 tablespoon (8 g) dried serrano peppers

2 tablespoons (15 g) dried onion

1 teaspoon dried garlic

1 tablespoon (8 g) Chili Powder (page 23)

1 tablespoon (8 g) cumin

½ teaspoon lime zest

1 tablespoon Veggie Stock Powder (page 15)

5 cups (1.25 L) water

Fresh limes and cilantro, optional, for serving

First, be sure to use dried ingredients that are dehydrated to your specific dehydrator's instructions.

Add the black beans, bell peppers, serrano peppers, onion. garlic, chili powder, cumin, lime zest, veggie stock powder and water to a large pot. Stir it up to incorporate, and bring it to a quick boil. Remove from the heat, and cover for 30 to 60 minutes to allow the ingredients to rehydrate.

Turn the burner back on to reheat, for about 5 minutes, stirring.

Serve it in bowls, and top with cilantro and wedges of lime, if desired.

Mushroom and Quinoa Soup

While this recipe calls for dried baby portabella mushrooms, it works with any of your preferred mushrooms, so feel free to incorporate a variety. The quinoa makes this nice and fluffy.

Makes 3 to 4 servings

1 cup (123 g) dried baby portabella mushrooms

2 tablespoons (15 g) dried onion

2 tablespoons (15 g) dried carrot

2 tablespoons (15 g) dried celery

1 teaspoon dried garlic

1 teaspoon dried basil

1 teaspoon dried thyme

Pinch of dried red pepper flakes

4 cups (950 ml) vegetable stock

½ cup (107 g) quinoa

1 cup (240 ml) water

1 teaspoon butter

Salt and pepper to taste

First, be sure to use dried ingredients that are dehydrated to your specific dehydrator's instructions.

Add the portabella mushrooms, onion, carrot, celery, garlic, basil, thyme, red pepper and vegetable stock to a large pot. Stir it up to incorporate, and bring it to a quick boil. Remove from the heat, and cover for 30 to 60 minutes to allow the ingredients to rehydrate.

In a separate pot, bring the quinoa, water and butter to a quick boil, then cover it and remove from the heat. Let it sit for 15 minutes, until the quinoa has absorbed the liquid.

Stir the quinoa into the mushroom mixture, and reheat on medium-low heat for about 5 minutes, stirring.

Serve in bowls and adjust to taste with salt and pepper.

Coconut Curry Soup

The combination of Vindaloo curry and sriracha makes this dish a bit spicy, but you can easily tamp down the heat level by substituting a milder curry to your preference. Another variation on this recipe is to lightly toast the coconut flakes in a dry pan for a few minutes to bring in a slightly nutty flavor.

Makes 3 to 4 servings

½ cup (62 g) dried red bell peppers

2 tablespoons (15 g) dried carrot

½ cup (62 g) dried broccoli

¼ cup (30 g) dried spinach

2 tablespoons (15 g) dried onion

1 teaspoon dried garlic

1 teaspoon dried ginger

1 teaspoon dried cilantro

1 tablespoon (8 g) Vindaloo curry powder

1 teaspoon lime zest

1 dried Sriracha "dot" (page 29) (or 1 teaspoon dried Sriracha)

2 tablespoons (15 g) dried coconut flakes

2 teaspoons (5 g) milk powder

6 cups (1.5 L) vegetable stock

8 ounces (230 g) rice noodles

3 to 4 tablespoons (45 to 60 ml) soy sauce

First, be sure to use dried ingredients that are dehydrated to your specific dehydrator's instructions.

Add the bell peppers, carrot, broccoli, spinach, onion, garlic, ginger, cilantro, curry powder, lime zest, Sriracha dot, coconut flakes, milk powder and vegetable stock to a large pot. Stir it up to incorporate, and bring it to a quick boil. Remove from the heat, and cover for 30 to 60 minutes to allow the ingredients to rehydrate.

In a separate pot, boil the rice noodles for about 12 to 14 minutes, or until the noodles are cooked to your liking. Drain, and add to the soup mixture.

Finish it by swirling in the soy sauce and simmering on medium-low heat for 5 minutes.

Creamy Carrot Soup

Ginger with hints of dried basil and dried rosemary turn an ordinary carrot soup into something special. You can eat this right away, but I like to leave the finished soup in the refrigerator overnight and heat it up the next day. The flavors blend together even more. For a homemade variation, try adding coconut milk for an even creamier version. If you're on the trail, rehydrated chicken jerky is a nice addition.

Makes 3 to 4 servings

1½ cups (184 g) dried carrots

2 tablespoons (15 g) dried onion

1 teaspoon dried garlic

1 teaspoon dried rosemary

1 teaspoon dried basil

½ teaspoon dried ginger

1 teaspoon dried chili flakes

5 cups (1.25 L) water or chicken broth

Salt and pepper to taste

First, be sure to use dried ingredients that are dehydrated to your specific dehydrator's instructions.

Add the carrots, onion, garlic, rosemary, basil, ginger, chili flakes and water to a large pot. Stir it up to incorporate, and bring it to a quick boil. Remove from the heat, and cover for 30 to 60 minutes to allow the ingredients to rehydrate.

Transfer the mixture to a food processor, and process until creamy and smooth. Season with salt and pepper.

Pour the soup back into the pot, and reheat on medium-low heat for about 5 minutes, stirring.

Cheesy Enchilada Soup

This one is highly satisfying, a recipe you'll find yourself going back to over and over again. All you need are your dried ingredients and cream cheese to swirl in at the end. So creamy, you are certain to love it.

Makes 3 to 4 servings

¼ cup (30 g) dried crumbled bell peppers

2 tablespoons (15 g) dried onion

1 teaspoon dried garlic

½ cup (62 g) dried tomatoes

½ cup (102 g) dried cooked black beans

½ cup (102 g) dried cooked corn

¼ cup (63 g) tomato sauce leather

1 tablespoon (8 g) Chili Powder (page 23)

½ teaspoon cumin

4 cups (950 ml) vegetable stock

Salt and pepper to taste

8 ounces (230 g) cream cheese

Fresh chopped green onion, for serving

First, be sure to use dried ingredients that are dehydrated to your specific dehydrator's instructions.

Add the bell peppers, onion, garlic, tomatoes, black beans, corn, tomato sauce leather, chili powder, cumin, vegetable stock, salt and pepper to a large pot. Stir it up to incorporate, and bring it to a quick boil. Remove from the heat, and cover for 30 to 60 minutes to allow the ingredients to rehydrate.

Turn the burner back on to reheat, and stir in the cream cheese. Keep stirring until the cheese melts and incorporates into the soup completely. Let it simmer on medium-low heat for about 10 minutes. Serve it up with fresh green onion sprinkled over the top.

CAMPING, HIKING AND EASY MEALS

Dehydration allows you to enjoy some of your favorite foods quickly and easily, and practically anywhere you'd like. All you need is water and basic utensils. It is ideal for camping and hiking trips, where weight is a factor. Dehydrated foods weigh very little, and can be packed into convenient bags that do not add burden to your backpacks.

After a long day on the trail, you can enjoy hearty, nutritious, satisfying meals that normally would require a kitchen. Devour a different meal each evening, like pasta with your favorite red sauce, spicy chili, even one of my very favorites, risotto. Who says you can't eat well in the wild? These types of meals can be prepared at home ahead of time, dehydrated then rehydrated with very little effort. You can also enjoy them at home. Oftentimes I like to make large batches of particular meals, enjoy some that evening, then dehydrate the rest to rehydrate later for a quick, effortless meal. It is the ultimate preserving tool.

Dehydrated foods are convenient because you can store each meal together in a single pack, either in single servings or for as many as you'll be feeding. Once you arrive at camp, simply boil up some water, and let the food rehydrate. In some cases, you can store your meal in different components, with your vegetable mixtures in one bag, sauce leathers in another and your carbohydrates, such as rice, couscous or noodles, in another. This way, you can mix and match ingredients at will and create something unique every time.

Vegetarian meals are simpler for long-term storage, though you can easily bring along dried meats or jerkies to include with your recipes. Just be sure to store dried meats separately in case of spoilage. A few pieces of chopped chicken or beef jerky would be a welcome addition to many of these meals. If you're rehydrating these at home, you can easily cook up your preferred protein while the meal is rehydrating to include with the final dish.

Aside from meals, I've also included some recipes for camping and hiking essentials that you can snack on along the trail for energy.

Storing Your Dehydrated Meals

Make sure your ingredients and full meals are dried completely. Store them in vacuum-sealed bags or airtight containers and keep in a cool, dark place. Properly dried foods can be kept for a year or longer this way, and even longer in the fridge or freezer, so if you have an upcoming trip, you have plenty of time to prepare your meals and snacks.

Pasta Arrabbiata

Arrabbiata in Italian means angry, which refers to the spiciness of the sauce. I like to make this recipe with extra spicy giardiniera, but the oils from the mixture don't translate well for dehydrating. This version, however, includes spicy red pepper flakes, and dehydrates perfectly. Bring it to the campground and enjoy some pasta with a kick.

Makes 4 servings

1 tablespoon (15 ml) extra virgin olive oil

1 large yellow onion, chopped

1 large Italian sweet pepper, chopped

3 cloves garlic, chopped

16 ounces (475 ml) tomato sauce

6 ounces (180 ml) tomato paste

1 cup (240 ml) chicken stock

2 tablespoons (5 g) chopped fresh parsley

2 tablespoons (5 g) chopped fresh basil

1 to 2 tablespoons (8 to 15 g) spicy red pepper flakes

Salt and pepper to taste

Water, enough to cook your pasta plus 1½ cups (350 ml) per 2 servings, for rehydrating

1 pound (450 g) spaghetti noodles, or any pasta to your preference

Grated Parmesan cheese, for serving

Heat the olive oil in a pan over medium heat. Cook the onion and sweet pepper for about 5 minutes to soften them up, then add in the garlic. Stir, and cook for about a minute, or until the garlic becomes fragrant.

Add the tomato sauce, tomato paste, chicken stock, herbs, red pepper, salt and black pepper. Give it all a stir.

Reduce the heat, and simmer for 20 minutes. You can let it simmer longer for more flavor to develop.

Remove your sauce from the heat, and let it cool. Divide it into two portions, and pour the sauce onto two separate leather trays or over parchment paper. Spread the sauce as evenly as possible, about ¼ inch (6 mm) thick.

Dehydrate at 135°F (57°C) for 10 to 12 hours, or until the sauce leather easily pulls away from the sheets. It should feel slightly flexible but easy to break apart. Let the leathers cool.

Store the sauce leather in sealed jars or sealable bags in a cool, dark place.

When you're ready to rehydrate the Arrabbiata sauce for your meal, get a pot of salted water boiling for the pasta. In another pot, add the sauce leather with 1½ cups (350 ml) of water per 2 servings, and bring to a quick boil. Reduce the heat, and let it simmer for 15 minutes, or until the sauce is completely rehydrated. Boil your noodles to al dente, and toss with the sauce.

Sprinkle on a bit of Parmesan cheese and enjoy!

Pasta Puttanesca

Bring some Italian to your campground. Puttanesca is a famous Italian sauce, reputedly named for so-called "Ladies of the Night" who would make this sauce to entice men into their abodes. It is a tomato sauce seasoned with capers, olives, anchovies and more. This recipe will make 8 servings, so portion it out accordingly. I like to divide it into fourths for four separate, 2-person meals.

Makes 8 servings

1 tablespoon (15 ml) extra virgin olive oil

1 large yellow onion, chopped

1 large Italian sweet pepper, chopped

6 ounces (168 g) chopped hot soppressata

4 cloves garlic, chopped

1 (2-ounce [56-g]) tin flat anchovy fillets, drained

1 teaspoon red pepper flakes

1 cup (180 g) green or black olives, chopped

3 tablespoons (30 g) capers, drained

60 ounces (1.75 L) crushed tomatoes, or 4 cans

3 tablespoons (8 g) chopped fresh parsley

2 tablespoons (5 g) chopped fresh basil

Black pepper to taste

Water, enough to cook your pasta plus 1½ cups (350 ml) per 2 servings, for rehydrating

Salt

1 pound (450 g) spaghetti noodles, or any pasta to your preference

Grated Parmesan cheese, for serving, if desired

Heat the olive oil in a pot over medium heat. Cook the onion and sweet pepper for about 5 minutes to soften them up, then add in the soppressata and garlic. Stir, and cook for about a minute, or until the garlic becomes fragrant.

Add in the anchovies, red pepper flakes and olives. Mash up the anchovies with a wooden spoon, and stir it all together.

Add the capers, tomatoes, parsley, basil and black pepper, and stir.

Cover the pot and cook for 15 to 20 minutes, allowing the tomatoes to break down and the flavors to incorporate. You can let it simmer longer for more flavor to develop. I let mine simmer over an hour.

Break up the tomatoes, and stir it into a rustic mix. Remove your sauce from the heat, and let it cool. Divide it into four portions, and pour the sauce onto four separate leather trays or over parchment paper. Spread the sauce as evenly as possible, about ¼ inch (6 mm) thick.

Dehydrate at 135°F (57°C) for 10 to 12 hours, or until the sauce leather easily pulls away from the sheets. It should feel slightly flexible, but easy to break apart. Let the leathers cool.

Store the sauce leather in sealed jars or sealable bags in a cool, dark place.

When you're ready to rehydrate the Puttanesca for your meal, get a pot of salted water boiling for the pasta. In another pot, add the sauce leather with 1½ cups (350 ml) of water per 2 servings, and bring it to a quick boil. Reduce the heat and let it simmer for 15 to 20 minutes, or until the sauce is completely rehydrated. Boil your noodles to al dente, and toss with the sauce.

Sprinkle on a bit of Parmesan cheese and enjoy!

Butternut Squash Risotto

Creamy risotto dehydrates easily, and rehydrates just as easily at home or at the campsite. This is a vegetarian version of the recipe, but you might consider including dried bacon jerky crumbles, dried pancetta or dried shrimp for protein. Extra shredded Parmesan cheese is always a nice addition to sprinkle over the top.

Makes 4 servings

1 tablespoon (15 ml) olive oil

1 medium onion, chopped

1 serrano pepper, chopped

3 cloves garlic, chopped

1 cup (190 g) Arborio rice

½ cup (120 ml) dry white wine

2½ cups (595 ml) chicken or vegetable stock, warmed

2 cups (300 g) cooked butternut squash

1 cup (90 g) shredded Parmesan cheese

Salt and pepper to taste

4 cups (950 ml) water or stock, for rehydrating

Heat the oil in a large pot to medium heat. Add the onion and serrano pepper, and cook for about 4 minutes to soften, then add the garlic and stir. Cook for about a minute, or until the garlic is nice and fragrant.

Add the rice and stir until completely combined. Next, add the wine and allow the rice to absorb the liquid, stirring often over gentle heat, for about 5 minutes.

Add the stock a half of a cup (120 ml) at a time, stirring often, until it is absorbed into the rice and the rice is soft and creamy. The entire process can take anywhere from 20 to 30 minutes, depending on how al dente you like your rice.

Stir in the cooked butternut squash and incorporate it into the rice. The overall mixture should be fairly smooth, with the rice tender but retaining its shape.

Remove from heat and stir in the Parmesan cheese. Add salt and pepper to taste.

Spread the risotto over a few dehydrator sheets, and dehydrate at 125°F (52°C) for 10 to 12 hours, or until the mixture is completely dried through. It will be crumbly, and will break apart very easily.

Cool and store the risotto in airtight containers or bags in a cool, dark place.

When you are ready to rehydrate at home or at the campground, add the dehydrated risotto to a large pot with the water. Stir it up to incorporate, and bring it to a quick boil. Remove from the heat and cover for 30 to 60 minutes to allow the ingredients to rehydrate.

Turn the burner back on to reheat for about 5 minutes, stirring.

Pea and Sunflower Seed Risotto

Peas and toasted sunflower seeds add dimension and depth to your favorite creamy risotto recipe. Bring along extra sunflower seeds to sprinkle over the top just before serving, if you'd like. Camping has never been so good! This risotto is perfect for both campsite cooking and for a quick meal at home. Dehydrated risotto, which only needs water to rehydrate, also makes for a great gift.

Makes 4 servings

2 tablespoons (30 g) butter

1 medium onion, chopped

1 cup (173 g) chopped jalapeño pepper, or use serrano to make it spicier, or bell pepper to tame the heat

3 cloves garlic, chopped

1 cup (190 g) Arborio rice

½ cup (120 ml) dry white wine

2½ cups (595 ml) chicken or vegetable stock, warmed

1 cup (150 g) frozen peas

½ cup (82 g) roasted sunflower seeds

1 cup (90 g) shredded Parmesan cheese

Salt and pepper to taste

4 cups (950 ml) water or stock, for rehydrating

Melt the butter in a large pot over medium heat. Add the onion and jalapeño peppers, and cook for 5 minutes to soften, then add the garlic and stir. Cook for about a minute, or until the garlic is nice and fragrant.

Add the rice and stir to completely combine. Next, add the wine and allow the rice to absorb the liquid, stirring often over gentle heat, for about 5 minutes.

Add the stock a half of a cup (120 ml) at a time, stirring often, until it is absorbed into the rice, and the rice is soft and creamy. The entire process can take anywhere from 20 to 30 minutes, depending on how al dente you like your rice.

Stir in the peas and roasted sunflower seeds, and incorporate the mixture into the rice. The overall consistency should be fairly smooth, with the rice tender but retaining its shape.

Remove from the heat, and stir in the Parmesan cheese. Add salt and pepper to taste.

Spread the risotto over a few dehydrator sheets, and dehydrate at 125°F (52°C) for 10 to 12 hours, or until the mixture is completely dried through. It will be crumbly, and will break apart very easily.

Cool and store the risotto in airtight containers or bags in a cool, dark place.

When you are ready to rehydrate at home or at the campground, add the dehydrated risotto to a large pot with the water. Stir it up to incorporate, and bring it to a quick boil. Remove from the heat, and cover for 30 to 60 minutes to allow the ingredients to rehydrate.

Turn the burner back on to reheat for about 5 minutes, stirring.

Coconut Chickpea Curry

Curry around the campfire? Yep! Prepare this meal completely ahead in your kitchen, dehydrate it and store it. Carry it along on your camping trip, and easily rehydrate it with water to enjoy your favorite curry dish, no matter where you are. This is a vegetarian version, but you can add dried shrimp or chicken jerky as desired.

Makes 2 servings, or more if using rice

2 tablespoons (30 ml) olive oil

1 large white onion, chopped

2 cloves garlic, chopped

1 (14-ounce [392-g]) can whole tomatoes, drained

1 (16-ounce [460-g]) can chickpeas, drained

1 tablespoon (8 g) garam masala

1 tablespoon (8 g) curry powder

½ teaspoon cumin

1 (14-ounce [392-g]) can coconut milk

Juice from 1 lime

Salt and pepper to taste

3 cups (720 ml) water or stock, for rehydrating

1 cup (190 g) dehydrated cooked rice, optional, for serving

Heat the oil in a large pot to medium heat. Add the onion, and cook for 4 minutes to soften, then add the garlic and stir. Cook for a minute, or until the garlic is nice and fragrant.

Add the tomatoes and break them apart with a wooden spoon. Simmer for 10 minutes, or until the tomatoes begin to break down and release their juices.

Stir in the chickpeas, garam masala, curry powder and cumin.

Add the coconut milk and lime juice, and stir it all to incorporate it. Bring the curry to a boil, then reduce the heat and simmer for 10 minutes to let the flavors develop.

Taste, and adjust with salt and pepper to your personal preference.

Spread the curry over a few dehydrator sheets, and dehydrate at 125°F (52°C) for 10 to 12 hours, or until the mixture is completely dried through. It will be crumbly, and will break apart very easily.

Cool and store the curry in airtight containers or bags in a cool, dark place. When you are ready to rehydrate at home or at the campground, add the dehydrated curry to a large pot with the water. Stir it up to incorporate, and bring it to a quick boil. Remove from the heat, and cover for 30 to 60 minutes to allow the ingredients to rehydrate.

Turn the burner back on to reheat for about 5 minutes, stirring. You can enjoy it as-is or serve it with rehydrated rice, if desired.

Red Beans and Rice

This meal is one that does not need to be prepared ahead and then dehydrated. Instead, you only need a collection of dried ingredients that come together into a cohesive, delicious meal. The only pre-cooking is for the rice and beans. Save time by using cooked, canned beans. Just be sure to drain them first. I call for vegetable stock here for rehydrating, but if you are on the trail, use water and dehydrated Veggie Stock Powder (page 15) instead.

Makes 3 to 4 servings

1 cup (204 g) dried cooked red kidney beans

1 cup (190 g) dried cooked white rice

¼ cup (30 g) dried crumbled jalapeño peppers

2 tablespoons (15 g) dried onion

1 teaspoon dried garlic

1 tablespoon (8 g) chipotle powder

1 teaspoon cumin

1 teaspoon dried cilantro

½ teaspoon dried lime zest

4 cups (950 ml) vegetable stock

Fresh chopped parsley and cilantro, optional, for serving

Add the beans, rice, jalapeño, onion, garlic, chipotle powder, cumin, cilantro, lime zest and stock to a large pot. Stir it up to incorporate, and bring it to a quick boil. Remove from the heat, and cover for 30 to 60 minutes to allow the ingredients to rehydrate.

Turn the burner back on to reheat, about 5 minutes, stirring. Serve it up with parsley and cilantro, if desired, sprinkled over the top.

Savory Red Bean Chili

There is no need to prepare your chili ahead and dehydrate. You can add a number of dehydrated ingredients together to form a simple, yet tasty, chili to be enjoyed at a campsite or at home from dried ingredients kept in your pantry.

Makes 3 to 4 servings

1 cup (204 g) dried cooked red kidney beans

¼ cup (30 g) dried crumbled poblano peppers

¼ cup (30 g) dried crumbled bell peppers

2 tablespoons (15 g) dried crumbled cayenne peppers

¼ cup (30 g) dried tomatoes

2 tablespoons (15 g) dried onion

2 ounces (56 g) tomato sauce leather

1 tablespoon (8 g) Chili Powder (page 23)

1 teaspoon dried garlic

1 teaspoon cumin

1 teaspoon dried basil

5 cups (1.25 L) vegetable stock

Add the beans, poblano peppers, bell peppers, cayenne peppers, tomatoes, onion, tomato sauce leather, chili powder, garlic, cumin, basil and stock to a large pot. Stir it up to incorporate, and bring it to a quick boil. Remove from the heat, and cover for 30 to 60 minutes to allow the ingredients to rehydrate.

Turn the burner back on to reheat for about 5 minutes, stirring.

Mexican-Style Couscous

Couscous is a quick meal dream, and an excellent alternative to rice. This meal does not need to be prepared ahead of time, but instead can be made by mixing various dried ingredients from your pantry. For camping, simply store them all together in a sealed baggie, and rehydrate when you're ready to eat. If you'd like to include a protein, store it separately. I suggest dried shrimp or chicken jerky.

Makes 3 to 4 servings

1 cup (190 g) dry couscous

1 tablespoon (8 g) dried garlic

1 tablespoon (8 g) dried crumbled jalapeño peppers

1 cup (204 g) dried cooked black beans

½ cup (62 g) dried crumbled tomatoes

¼ cup (51 g) dried corn

1 teaspoon Chili Powder (page 23)

½ teaspoon cumin

1 teaspoon dried lime

Salt and pepper to taste

5 cups (1.25 L) water or vegetable stock for rehydrating

First, be sure to use dried ingredients that are dehydrated to your specific dehydrator's instructions.

Add couscous, garlic, jalapeño peppers, black beans, tomatoes, corn, chili powder, cumin, lime, salt and pepper to a large pot with the water or vegetable stock. Stir it up to incorporate, and bring it to a quick boil. Remove from the heat, and cover for 30 to 60 minutes to allow the ingredients to rehydrate.

Turn the burner back on to reheat for about 5 minutes, stirring.

Cinnamon-Banana Oatmeal

Get your day started before a big hike with a hearty breakfast, filled with oatmeal and banana. Sweetened with a bit of cinnamon and brown sugar, you'll be set for the day with plenty of energy. For this recipe, you'll cook the steel cut oats completely first, then rehydrate later when you're ready to eat. The oats can be cooked at camp, but cooking them first at home, then dehydrating, will make for a much quicker meal.

Makes 2 servings

½ cup (90 g) steel cut oats

2½ cups (595 ml) water

1 cup (125 g) dried banana slices

2 tablespoons (23 g) brown sugar

1 tablespoon (8 g) cinnamon

1½ to 2 cups (350 to 475 ml) water, for rehydrating

First, be sure to use dried ingredients that are dehydrated to your specific dehydrator's instructions.

Add the steel cut oats and water to a pot. Bring it to a quick boil, then reduce the heat and simmer for about 30 minutes, or until the oats cook through completely. Cool it down, and then spread the cooked oatmeal out on a dehydrator sheet. Dry at 130°F (55°C) for 8 to 10 hours, or until completely dried through.

Cool and store the cooked oats, along with dried banana slices, brown sugar and cinnamon, in an airtight container or bag in a cool, dark cupboard.

When you are ready to rehydrate at home or at the campground, add the dried contents to a large pot with the water. Stir it up to incorporate, and bring it to a quick boil. Remove from the heat, and cover for 5 to 10 minutes to allow the ingredients to rehydrate.

Pineapple-Pear-Pecan Trail Mix

There are numerous ingredients you can use to make trail mix, including a huge variety of nuts, dried fruits, cereals and even chocolates or other sweets. This is a simple version that I personally enjoy. I took a small batch of this to a hiking trip in the Grand Canyon down the Bright Angel Trail. It didn't last long enough. I should have made more!

Makes 3 to 4 cups (360 to 480 g)

1 pineapple

3 pears

Lemon juice

1 cup (123 g) pecans

1 tablespoon (8 g) dried ginger powder

1 teaspoon red chili flakes

1 tablespoon (20 g) salt

First, be sure to use dried ingredients that are dehydrated to your specific dehydrator's instructions.

Peel and core the pineapple. Slice it into rings about ¼ inch (6 mm) thick, and then quarter the slices. Spread them out on dehydrator trays.

Slice the pears into ¼-inch (6-mm) thick slices, and remove the core and seeds. Spray them with a bit of lemon juice, and spread them out on dehydrator sheets.

Dry the pineapple and pear slices at 125°F (52°C) for 8 to 12 hours, or until the fruit is completely dried through. Each will feel papery, and the pears will snap in half when bent.

Tear the pineapple and pear slices into pieces then add to a mixing bowl along with the pecans, ginger powder, chili flakes and salt. Toss it to combine. Store the trail mix in airtight bags until your big hike.

Chocolate-Strawberry Power Bars

While this energy bar may seem more like a sweet snack, it is actually filled with loads of healthy, nutritious ingredients, including muesli, sunflower seeds, sweet strawberries and bananas, all made chocolaty with hazelnut spread. Perfect for the trail, but I also make it for snacking. These are not spicy, though you can easily add a spicy element to bring some heat.

Makes 12 square bars

1 cup (90 g) muesli

1 cup (240 ml) water

1 cup (123 g) dried strawberries

½ cup (62 g) dried banana

2 tablespoons (20 g) sunflower seeds

¼ cup (60 ml) honey

3 tablespoons (45 ml) chocolate hazelnut spread, such as Nutella

First, be sure to use dried ingredients that are dehydrated to your specific dehydrator's instructions.

Add the muesli and water to a large bowl, and let it soak for 30 minutes. Add the remaining ingredients, and mix with a wooden spoon. It should be rather loose.

Set the mixture onto a dehydrator sheet or parchment paper, and smooth it down until it is about ¼ inch (6 mm) thick. Dehydrate at 125°F (52°C) for 12 to 14 hours, or until completely dried through. It will remain somewhat sticky from the honey.

Slice into 1½-inch (3.8-cm) squares, and store in airtight containers.

Chewy Power Bars

Give yourself a burst of energy on the hiking trail with these nutritious power bars, made with crunchy muesli, sunflower seeds, coconut and apples. Honey sweetens the bars and helps bind them together. These are so much better than a store-bought granola bar. These are not spicy, though you can easily add a spicy element to bring some heat.

Makes 12 square bars

2 cups (120 g) dried apples, chopped
1 cup (90 g) muesli
2 tablespoons (20 g) sunflower seeds
2 tablespoons (15 g) dried coconut flakes
½ cup (120 ml) honey

First, be sure to use dried ingredients that are dehydrated to your specific dehydrator's instructions.

Add the apples, muesli, sunflower seeds and dried coconut flakes to a food processor. Process until it is combined and a bit chunky, and starts to powder. It will still retain much of its texture. Pour the powder into a bowl and add the honey. Mix it all together with a wooden spoon. It should be nice and sticky at this point.

Set the mixture onto a dehydrator sheet, and roll it down with a rolling pin until it is spread out to about ¼ inch (6 mm) thick. Top it with wax paper before rolling to avoid sticking to the rolling pin. Toss away the wax paper, and dehydrate at 125°F (52°C) for 10 hours, or until completely dried through. It will remain somewhat sticky from the honey.

Slice into 1½-inch (3.8-cm) squares, and store in airtight containers.

Nutty Strawberry-Peach Energy Leather

This will keep you going on the trail, with plenty of strawberries, peach, blueberries, pecans and sunflower seeds, all rolled up into a simple leather. It is very portable, and can be cut into strips, rolled or easily folded. These are not spicy, though you can easily add a spicy element to bring some heat.

Makes 3 leathers

2 cups (300 g) chopped strawberries
1 cup (150 g) chopped peach
1 teaspoon lemon juice
2 tablespoons (30 ml) honey
½ cup (75 g) chopped blueberries
½ cup (82 g) sunflower seeds
½ cup (62 g) chopped pecans

Add the strawberries, peach, lemon juice and honey to a pot and bring to a simmer. Cook the mixture for about 10 minutes, or until the fruit starts to soften and break down. Cool the fruit mixture, then add it to a food processor and process it until smooth. Stir in the blueberries, sunflower seeds and pecans.

Spread it over a dehydrator leather tray or drying sheet to ¼-inch (6-mm) thickness. I use a spoon to spread it out as evenly as possible, 1 cup (240 ml) per sheet. This will help it dehydrate more evenly.

Dehydrate at 130°F (54°C) for 6 to 8 hours, or until the leather peels away from the tray easily. You might need to use a knife to get along the edges, as it will be tacky, but it should not stick too much.

Flip the leather and dehydrate for 2 hours, or until it is completely dry and there aren't any moist spots left.

Cool it down a bit, and then roll it up. You can enjoy your leather now, or wrap in plastic wrap and store in a cool, dry place. It will keep for 6 months or longer.

SNACKS AND MUNCHIES

Growing up, I was pretty bad about snacking. I would binge on sweets, bags of potato chips and other questionable foods far more often than I should have. As I grew older, and the waistline began to expand, I worked on giving up on those poorly chosen snack foods and replacing them with healthier choices.

Lucky for me, I now have a dehydrator!

You can use your dehydrator to make healthy, homemade snacks that can be enjoyed any time, and they're far healthier than what you can grab from the store aisles. You can easily make your own crunchy snacks, sweet bites and tasty desserts where you control the ingredients.

For some snacks, there is no need for rehydrating. Dried snacks such as veggie chips or watermelon treats offer a pleasant crunch or chewiness and natural sweetness that can be enhanced with other ingredients, or easily spiced and flavored. Not only are dried snacks convenient, but also they lack the preservatives of store bought snacks, so they help promote a healthier lifestyle.

Other snacks can be rehydrated quickly and enjoyed as quick bites or desserts, such as rice pudding or other fruity desserts.

Spiced Cauliflower Popcorn

Cauliflower dehydrates to crumbly little bites that are reminiscent of popcorn. Because of its mild flavor, you can introduce any flavors you'd like. I enjoy my snacks with a spicy kick, so I've used hot sauce along with chili powder, though you can adapt this to your own tastes.

Makes 1½ cups (340 g)

1 head cauliflower
3 tablespoons (45 ml) coconut oil
¼ cup (60 ml) hot sauce
1 tablespoon (8 g) paprika
1 teaspoon smoked cayenne
½ teaspoon cumin
Salt and pepper to taste

Rinse the cauliflower, and chop the florets into bites slightly larger than popcorn. Toss them in a large bowl with the coconut oil, hot sauce, paprika, cayenne, cumin, salt and pepper. Get them nicely coated with all the seasonings. Taste, and add in a few more dashes of hot sauce, if needed.

Spread the mixture out onto dehydrator trays, and dehydrate for 8 to 12 hours at 130°F (54°C), or until they are completely dried through. You can eat them when they are not completely dried, but they will be chewier. Drying all the way through will result in crunchier, popcorn-like texture.

Store the popcorn in a cool, dry place in airtight baggies.

Salted Mint Watermelon Treats

Give me the combination of salt and watermelon any day of the week. With a dehydrator, you can enjoy the flavors of summer any time of year. Mint and lime add a dash of brightness, and the flavor is quite concentrated. The watermelon slices shrink down to almost a fruit leather–like quality, so you can roll them up if you'd like, or eat them as they are.

Makes 2 cups (300 g)

1 small seedless watermelon

Juice from 1 large lime

1 tablespoon (20 g) salt, or more as desired

2 tablespoons (15 g) dried ground mint

1 teaspoon spicy Chili Powder (page 23)

Slice the watermelon in half, and then into ¼-inch (6-mm) pieces.

Remove the rinds and discard them. I like to make large pieces for this recipe.

Drizzle the slices with lime juice, and then sprinkle generously with salt and dried mint. Flip, and repeat.

Set them onto the dehydrator sheets. Dehydrate at 135°F (57°C) for about 12 hours, then peel and flip them once they are mostly dried through. Dehydrate for 4 hours, or until they are nicely dried through. They should be a bit pliable when they're done.

Store them in a cool, dry place in airtight baggies.

Cinnamon-Mint Pears

When dehydrated, pears make sweet, slightly chewy snacks that are highly portable. Toss them into baggies, carry them around in your pocket or stash them away in your handbag. They're great on their own, but when seasoned with citrus, cinnamon and dried mint, they become something amazing unto themselves.

Makes 20 chips

2 Bartlett pears

Juice from 1 blood orange, or other oranges, if desired

1 tablespoon (8 g) ground cinnamon

1 tablespoon (8 g) dried ground mint

Slice the pears into ¼-inch (6-mm) pieces, and remove the seeds. Toss the slices in a large bowl with the blood orange juice, and then sprinkle each slice with cinnamon and mint. Toss to make sure each piece is evenly coated on both sides.

Set them onto the dehydrator sheets. Dehydrate at 135°F (57°C) for about 12 hours, or until they are nicely dried through. They should be a bit pliable when they're done.

Store the pears in a cool, dry place in airtight baggies.

Spiced Chickpeas

Spiced chickpeas, or garbanzo beans, make for a tasty, natural, crunchy snack with just the right amount of kick. I prefer using fresh chickpeas that I can cook myself, but this recipe also works with canned chickpeas; so if you're unable to find the fresh kind, give the canned product a try.

Makes 1 cup (150 g)

2 cups (300 g) cooked chickpeas
2 tablespoons (30 ml) Sriracha sauce
1 teaspoon paprika
½ teaspoon cayenne powder
½ teaspoon granulated garlic
½ teaspoon dried basil
Dash of salt

Toss the chickpeas, Sriracha, paprika, cayenne powder, garlic, basil and salt together in a large mixing bowl. Make sure the chickpeas are evenly coated.

Spread them out evenly onto the dehydrator sheets. Dehydrate at 125°F (52°C) for about 10 hours, or until they are nicely dried through. They should be slightly crunchy when they're done.

Store the chickpeas in a cool, dry place in airtight baggies.

Sweet Mixed Berry Rice Pudding

Arborio rice is the main ingredient in Italian risotto. Who would think it could make a sweet dessert? Because of the creaminess of the cooked rice, it breaks down into a pudding-like texture that mixes perfectly with sweeter flavors. This version is loaded with tart berries.

Makes 2 servings

¼ cup (48 g) dried cooked Arborio rice
¼ cup (30 g) dried blueberries
¼ cup (30 g) dried raspberries
2 tablespoons (23 g) brown sugar
1 teaspoon salt
½ tablespoon (4 g) cinnamon
¾ cup (60 ml) water, for rehydrating
Fresh raspberries, for serving, if desired

First, be sure to use dried ingredients that are dehydrated to your specific dehydrator's instructions.

Store the rice, blueberries, dried raspberries, brown sugar, salt and cinnamon in an airtight bag or jar until ready to use.

When you're ready for a sweet snack, add the rice, blueberries, dried raspberries, brown sugar, salt, cinnamon and water to a small pot and stir. Bring it to a quick boil, then reduce heat and simmer slightly until the mixture is rehydrated, stirring often.

Top with fresh raspberries, if desired, and enjoy!

Pineapple-Mango Dessert

When you're in the mood for a taste of the tropics, this recipe will bring you back to the ocean. The pineapple and mango rehydrate to a compote-like consistency, which can be enjoyed with a spoon. It's sweetened a bit more with sugar, with a touch of mint for brightness.

Makes 2 servings

½ cup (62 g) dried pineapple

½ cup (62 g) dried mango

1 tablespoon (13 g) granulated sugar

1 teaspoon dried mint, plus a dash for serving

1 tablespoon (8 g) cornstarch

1 cup (240 ml) water, for rehydrating

First, be sure to use dried ingredients that are dehydrated to your specific dehydrator's instructions.

Store the pineapple, mango, sugar, mint and cornstarch in an airtight bag or jar until ready to use.

When you're ready to rehydrate, add the pineapple, mango, sugar, mint and cornstarch to a small pot, and stir with the water. Bring it to a quick boil, then reduce heat and simmer slightly until the mixture is rehydrated, stirring often. Cool and top with extra dried mint flakes.

Nectarine-Raspberry Dessert

Dehydrated fruits can be rehydrated to a compote-like consistency, ideal for a quick dessert. The cornstarch thickens it up just enough, and the combination of cinnamon and brown sugar adds a touch of sweetness.

Makes 2 servings

½ cup (62 g) dried nectarine slices
¼ cup (30 g) dried raspberries
2 tablespoons (23 g) brown sugar
1 tablespoon (8 g) cornstarch
½ teaspoon cinnamon
Dash of salt
1 cup (240 ml) water, for rehydrating
Crumbled walnuts, for serving

First, be sure to use dried ingredients that are dehydrated to your specific dehydrator's instructions.

Store the nectarine slices, raspberries, brown sugar, cornstarch, cinnamon and salt in an airtight bag or jar until ready to use.

When you're ready to rehydrate, add the nectarine slices, raspberries, brown sugar, cornstarch, cinnamon and salt to a small pot, and stir with the water. Bring it to a quick boil, then reduce heat and simmer slightly until the mixture is rehydrated, stirring often. Cool and top with crumbled walnuts, if desired.

Chocolate-Banana Dessert

Chocolate and banana are one of life's classic flavor pairings and always satisfy for dessert. Dehydrated bananas have a very creamy quality when rehydrated. I enjoy adding dried coconut flakes, which you can toast ahead of time if you'd prefer a nuttier flavor.

Makes 2 servings

2 dried sliced bananas

1 heaping teaspoon cocoa powder

¼ cup (30 g) dried coconut

1 tablespoon (8 g) cornstarch

2 tablespoons (23 g) brown sugar

½ teaspoon cinnamon

Dash of salt

1 cup (240 ml) water, for rehydrating

Slivered almonds, for serving

Dried coconut, for serving

First, be sure to use dried ingredients that are dehydrated to your specific dehydrator's instructions.

Store the bananas, cocoa powder, coconut, cornstarch, brown sugar, cinnamon and salt in an airtight bag or jar until ready to use.

When you're ready to rehydrate, add the bananas, cocoa powder, coconut, cornstarch, brown sugar, cinnamon and salt to a small pot, and stir with the water. Bring it to a quick boil, then reduce heat and simmer slightly until the mixture is rehydrated, stirring often. Cool and top with slivered almonds and extra dried coconut.

Wicked Veggie Chips

Ditch the fried potato chips and opt for a mix of crunchy, slightly spicy dried vegetable chips that will satisfy your munchie craving. I enjoy a mixture of carrots and zucchini, though there are numerous vegetables you might include. The seasoning is spicy from the hot sauce, though you can use a milder sauce brand for chips with less heat. Use a brand to your personal tastes.

Makes 2 cups (70 g)

1 pound (450 g) carrots

1 pound (450 g) zucchini

6 ounces (180 ml) of your favorite hot sauce, plus more for serving, if desired

Bring a large pot of water to boil.

Peel and wash the carrots, and then slice them into ¼-inch (6-mm) slices. Boil them for 5 minutes, then immediately plunge them into ice water to stop them from cooking. Cool, and then add them to a large mixing bowl.

Slice the zucchini into ¼-inch (6-mm) slices, and add them to the mixing bowl. Add hot sauce and toss to combine. Make sure everything is evenly coated with the hot sauce.

Spread the slices out on dehydrator trays, and dehydrate at 125°F (52°C) for 10 to 12 hours, or until they are completely dried through. They should be brittle and snap in half when bent.

Store in airtight containers.

You can enjoy them as they are, or toss them with a bit more hot sauce when you're ready to eat them for extra spice and flavor.

Zesty Potato Matchsticks

Get your crunchy-munchie fix with these potato matchsticks that have been seasoned with a mixture of spices and then dehydrated to perfection. You'll never want for store-bought munchies again. Homemade is so much better.

Makes 3 cups (120 g)

2 pounds (900 g) yellow potatoes
2 tablespoons (30 ml) lemon juice
1 teaspoon dried mustard
1 teaspoon ancho powder
1 teaspoon garlic powder
1 teaspoon onion powder
½ teaspoon turmeric
Salt and pepper to taste

Peel the potatoes and slice them into thin matchsticks. You'll want them ¼-inch (6-mm) thick, maximum. The thinner they are, the faster they will dehydrate, and the crunchier they will be.

Add them to a large mixing bowl, and toss them with the lemon juice. This will keep them from darkening during the drying process.

Add the mustard, ancho powder, garlic powder, onion powder, turmeric, salt and pepper, and toss the matchsticks to coat everything nicely.

Spread the seasoned matchsticks over dehydrator sheets, and dry them at 125°F (52°C) for 6 to 8 hours, or until they are completely dried through. It helps to stir them up a bit after a few hours to dry more quickly. They should finish very dry and brittle.

Store them in an airtight container in a cool, dark place.

Sweet and Spicy Sweet Potato Chips

These sweet potato chips may look like regular potato chips, but they're really quite different. They're much crunchier in consistency. You can slice them thicker to enjoy a crunchy bite with more "chew" and substance to it, but I prefer them sliced as thinly as possible. You will still get plenty of crunch factor, as well as sweetness from the butter pecan maple syrup.

Makes 3 cups (130 g)

2 pounds (900 g) sweet potatoes

¼ cup (60 ml) butter pecan maple syrup

1 teaspoon ground cinnamon

1 teaspoon sea salt

Peel the sweet potatoes and slice them into thin chips, about ¼-inch (6-mm) thick, maximum. The thinner they are, the faster they will dehydrate, and the crunchier they will be.

Add them to a large mixing bowl, and toss them with the maple syrup, ground cinnamon and salt. Get them all completely coated. You can add more seasoning if you'd like.

Spread the seasoned potato chips over dehydrator sheets, and dry them at 125°F (52°C) for 6 to 10 hours, or until they are completely dried through. It helps to stir them up a bit after a few hours to dry more quickly. They should finish very dry and brittle.

Store them in an airtight container in a cool, dark place.

DRINKS AND INFUSIONS

I became interested in infusing liquids by way of my food blog and my garden. We grow numerous chili peppers each year, and I wanted to make my own chili oils. Infusing oils with fresh chili peppers is not a good idea, as the peppers can grow rancid and ruin the whole thing. Lucky for me, I owned a dehydrator, which I had already been using to make my own powders and seasoning blends.

Soon I was infusing any liquid I could think of as a way of experimenting and learning what works and what doesn't. Of course, you can infuse liquids with fresh ingredients, and often you may want to, but dehydrated ingredients are superior to fresh ingredients in many ways for infusing liquids with flavors.

Dehydrated ingredients infuse faster because they absorb the liquid, and their flavor disperses more quickly. They are also less messy, as all the work is already done, and you can simply pluck your ingredients from your pantry and infuse at will.

You can infuse anything for flavor, from water to oil to beer and other alcohols. You only need to peruse the local liquor store aisles to see the popularity of infused alcohols, with an incredible choice of flavor combinations. Now you can make them at home whenever you'd like.

Making Tea Blends

Your dehydrator is ideal for making your own tea blends. You now have the opportunity to create blends you'd never find in any store. With an entire world of herbs, fruits, spices and more, you are limited only by your creativity. You can keep individual ingredients on hand in your pantry to mix together at a moment's notice. I prefer using a small tea infuser for making individual servings, though larger mesh tea balls are ideal for larger batches.

For making tea, all you need to do is combine 2 to 3 tablespoons (15 to 23 g) of your preferred mix in a tea infuser, and steep it in boiling water for about 5 minutes. Done!

Store your tea blends in airtight containers in a cool, dark place. They will last 6 months or longer in the pantry, and up to a year in the freezer.

Here are just a few ideas to help get you started.

Ginger Lemon Tea

Ginger and lemon are a classic combination, and make for a light, flavorful tea blend. This is one of my favorite go-to blends in the summer. Enjoy it hot, but it works just as well on ice.

Makes 1 serving

1 tablespoon (8 g) dried ginger flakes
1 tablespoon (8 g) crushed dried lemon
½ teaspoon dried thyme
½ teaspoon dried rosemary

First, be sure to use dried ingredients that are dehydrated to your specific dehydrator's instructions.

Fill your tea infuser with the ginger, lemon, thyme and rosemary. Bring water to a boil, and pour it into a thick teacup. Steep the tea blend in the hot water for 5 to 10 minutes to let the flavors permeate.

Apple Pie Tea

Some of your favorite apple pie ingredients come together for the perfect autumn tea blend, with a strong apple flavor. Honey adds just the right amount of sweet. This blend is great with ice cream.

Makes 1 serving

1 tablespoon (8 g) dried apple powder, or dried apple peels

½ teaspoon ground cinnamon

½ teaspoon ground nutmeg

1 teaspoon honey

First, be sure to use dried ingredients that are dehydrated to your specific dehydrator's instructions.

Fill your tea infuser with the apple powder, cinnamon, nutmeg and honey. Bring water to a boil, and pour it into a thick teacup. Steep the tea blend in the hot water for 5 to 10 minutes to let the flavors permeate.

Orange Chili Tea

This is definitely a combination for those who enjoy a bit of heat. The spiciness from the dried chili flakes brings a warm, blooming heat that lingers. You can easily adjust the heat level based on your choice of peppers. Enjoy this blend with a spicy brunch.

Makes 1 serving

1 tablespoon (8 g) crushed dried orange

1 tablespoon (8 g) crushed dried red chili

¼ tablespoon (2 g) whole black peppercorns

1 teaspoon honey

First, be sure to use dried ingredients that are dehydrated to your specific dehydrator's instructions.

Fill your tea infuser with the orange, chili, peppercorns and honey. Bring water to a boil, and pour it into a thick teacup. Steep the tea blend in the hot water for 5 to 10 minutes to let the flavors permeate.

Infused Oils

Infused oils are essential to many cuisines around the world. Making them at home is a snap with dehydrated ingredients. I often use chili oil in dishes such as noodles or stir-fries, and for drizzling as a finisher. Other ingredients you can use include garlic, shallots, peppercorns, ginger root and so much more. Get as creative as you'd like to your own flavor preferences. A neutral oil is best for making oils, as it will highlight the flavors of your infusions better.

Simple Chili Oil

Here is a recipe for a simple chili oil that I enjoy using at home. You can also include whole, dried chili peppers in the oil, which can be decorative.

Makes 1 cup (240 ml)

1 cup (240 ml) vegetable oil

3 tablespoons (23 g) or more crushed dried chili peppers

Dash of salt, optional

First, be sure to use dried ingredients that are dehydrated to your specific dehydrator's instructions.

Add the vegetable oil, crushed chili peppers and salt, if using, to a small pot and stir. Heat over medium-low heat, and stir often for about 15 minutes. Do not allow the oil to smoke or boil. If it smokes, remove it from the heat to reduce the temperature. You really just want to have a nice slow simmer.

After 15 minutes, remove from the heat and let the oil cool. Pour it into a bottle or jar. You can strain it if you'd like.

Store the oil in the refrigerator in an airtight jar. It is best used within a month or two.

Herbed Chili Oil

You can easily infuse your chili oils with dried herbs to use as a finisher. I find this particular recipe works best with Italian foods.

Makes 1 cup (240 ml)

1 cup (240 ml) vegetable oil

2 tablespoons (16 g) or more crushed dried chili peppers

1 teaspoon dried basil

1 teaspoon dried oregano

½ teaspoon dried thyme

½ teaspoon black peppercorns

Dash of salt, if desired

First, be sure to use ingredients that are dehydrated to your specific dehydrator's instructions.

Add the vegetable oil, crushed chili peppers, basil, oregano, thyme, peppercorns and salt (if using) to a small pot and stir. Heat to medium-low and stir often for about 15 minutes. Do not allow the oil to smoke or boil. If it smokes, remove it from the heat to reduce the temperature. You really just want to have a nice slow simmer.

After 15 minutes, remove from heat and let the oil cool. Pour it into a bottle or jar. You can strain it if you'd like.

Store in the refrigerator in an airtight jar. It is best used within a month or two.

Chinese-Style Chili Oil

I use this particular oil as a starter for sautéing my vegetables, then as a finisher by drizzling the colorful oil over the final dish. You get a double whammy of flavor this way.

Makes 1 cup (240 ml)

1 cup (240 ml) vegetable oil

2 tablespoons (16 g) or more crushed dried chili peppers

1 teaspoon dried ginger

1 bay leaf

2 star anise

1 teaspoon dried scallions

1 teaspoon dried garlic

½ teaspoon Sichuan peppercorns

Dash of salt, if desired

First, be sure to use ingredients that are dehydrated to your specific dehydrator's instructions.

Add the vegetable oil, crushed chili peppers, ginger, bay leaf, star anise, scallions, garlic, peppercorns and salt (if using) to a small pot and stir. Heat to medium-low and stir often for about 15 minutes. Do not allow the oil to smoke or boil. If it smokes, remove it from the heat to reduce the temperature. You really just want to have a nice slow simmer.

After 15 minutes, remove from heat and let the oil cool. Pour it into a bottle or jar. You can strain it if you'd like.

Store in the refrigerator in an airtight jar. It is best used within a month or two.

Cucumber-Lemon Water

Hot summer days and pleasant brunches call for cool, refreshing glasses of water. With dehydrated ingredients, you can serve up a flavored pitcher of water in practically no time. Because they are dried, the ingredients will flavor the water much more quickly than fresh ingredients. This recipe, infused with lemon and cucumber, is a tasty combination.

Makes 1 pitcher, 3 quarts

1 dehydrated sliced lemon
1 dehydrated sliced cucumber
1 pitcher of water (3 quarts)

First, be sure to use dried ingredients that are dehydrated to your specific dehydrator's instructions.

Add the dehydrated lemon and cucumbers to a pitcher of ice-cold water. Let it sit for 10 minutes for a mild flavor, or longer for a more potent flavor.

Infusing Alcohols

Alcohols of any type take on the flavors of dehydrated ingredients very quickly. Now that you have a dehydrator in your possession, you are no longer limited to the expensive, chemical-based flavor combinations available at your local liquor store.

Mid- to high-quality alcohols are better for infusing, as no amount of dried ingredients will raise the bar of a cheap, low-level alcohol. Higher proof alcohols will pull more flavors from the dried ingredients, so plan accordingly. Any alcohol is fair game with infusing. Whether you prefer vodka, bourbon, tequila, rum, gin, or even beer and wine, there is a flavor combination waiting for you.

The amount of time you allow your booze to soak with the dried ingredients is up to you. I recommend at least 12 hours, but realistically, you can infuse alcohols almost indefinitely this way. I don't like to infuse for too long, as the dried foods can break down and float around, depending on the ingredients you've chosen to work with. I've found that a few days of soaking time is ideal for most alcohols, but again, test along the way and strain out the ingredients when you've achieved your preferred results.

Once again, it is time to get creative and follow your palate's desire. Typical ingredients for infusing alcohol, depending on your booze of choice, include fruits, vegetables, nuts, herbs and spices of all types.

Infused liquors also make thoughtful gifts. Here are a few simple combinations we love at home.

Bacon Infused Vodka

If you're a Blood Mary fan, you will love this infusion. A bit of bacon makes everything better.

Makes 16 ounces (475 ml)

16 ounce (475 ml) jar with lid
2 to 3 pieces of bacon jerky
Your favorite brand of unflavored vodka

Set the bacon jerky into your jar and fill it up with vodka. Make sure to use enough vodka to cover the bacon.

Tightly seal the jar with the lid and store in a cool, dark place, away from direct sunlight.

The bacon will begin to infuse right away, but it is best to et it sit for at least 12 hours for a more full-flavored infusion. You can leave it for several days if you'd like.

Strain the vodka into a separate container. Cheesecloth helps strain out any particulates you might have. Toss away the bacon.

Finally, transfer your infused vodka into clean glass jars or bottles, and seal them up. Infused vodkas will keep indefinitely.

Apple Infused Bourbon

Bourbon fans can sip this apple-flavored bourbon on its own, or use it as a base for new and interesting cocktails.

Makes 16 ounces (475 ml)

16 ounce (475 ml) jar with lid
1 cup (60 g) dehydrated apple slices
Your favorite brand of unflavored bourbon

First, be sure to use dried ingredients that are dehydrated to your specific dehydrator's instructions.

Set the apple slices into the bottom of your jar and fill it up with bourbon. Make sure to use enough bourbon to cover the apples.

Tightly seal the jar with the lid and store in a cool, dark place, away from direct sunlight.

The apple will begin to infuse right away, but it is best to let it sit for at least 12 hours for a more full-flavored infusion. You can leave it for several days if you'd like.

Strain the bourbon into a separate container. Cheesecloth helps strain out any particulates you might have. Toss away the apples.

Finally, transfer your infused bourbon into clean glass jars or bottles, and seal them up. Infused bourbons will keep indefinitely.

*See photo on page 170.

Tropical Fruit Infused Rum

I fell in love with pineapple and coconut rums in the Florida Keys, where they were everywhere. Now that I make my own, I enjoy infusing rum with BOTH flavors together. These flavors make excellent cocktails.

Makes 16 ounces (475 ml)

16 ounce (475 ml) jar with lid
½ cup (62 g) dehydrated coconut flakes
½ cup (62 g) dehydrated pineapple slices
Your favorite brand of unflavored rum

First, be sure to use dried ingredients that are dehydrated to your specific dehydrator's instructions.

Set the coconut flakes and pineapple into your jar and fill it up with rum. Make sure to use enough rum to cover the dried fruit.

Tightly seal the jar with the lid and store in a cool, dark place, away from direct sunlight.

The fruit will begin to infuse right away, but it is best to let it sit for at least 12 hours for a more full-flavored infusion. You can leave it for several days if you'd like.

Strain the rum into a separate container. Cheesecloth helps strain out any particulates you might have. Toss away the fruit.

Finally, transfer your infused rum into clean glass jars or bottles, and seal them up. Infused rum will keep indefinitely.

*See photo on page 170.

PRACTICALS

As a cook, you will always have items that are typically thrown away. Creative cooks learn ways to use some of those ingredients. I have a number of tricks I've learned over the years that, in retrospect, I wish I'd learned long ago.

For example: Parmesan cheese rinds. You can add them to tomato sauces, and simmer them to infuse their flavor. I can't think of a tomato sauce that wouldn't benefit from a bit of Parmesan cheese, and what a phenomenal way to use an ingredient you might normally throw away. I've also used the cheese rind for stock making. It adds a new flavor element to the stock.

Speaking of stocks, I like to save pieces of the vegetables you might normally compost or throw away for stock making. Items like asparagus stems and herb stems are still useful, and filled with enough nutrients to make an excellent stock. The same goes for shrimp shells, which can be used to make homemade seafood stock. Use lobster and crab shells the same way. Your soups and sauces will never be the same.

Why waste anything that you can reuse to smart effect? Once you begin thinking in that direction, it's hard to go back. Seriously, who would think that nut shells could be useful to anyone? What about fruit rinds and peels? Yep, I like to dehydrate citrus peels of all types—apple peels, pear peels, pineapple peels, coconut shells, you name it. See below for how I like to use them.

Are you a craft beer maker? Do you enjoy home brewing? Did you realize all those spent grains, which are integral to making beer, can have a new life? Yes. Check out some of the recipes in this chapter to see how.

How to Make Potpourri from Discarded Ingredients

Potpourri is a mixture of dried items, such as flowers, pine cones, tree bark and spices that help scent a room. It is often decorative, placed in ornate bowls or other containers. You can make it from numerous items at hand to your own preference, which makes your dehydrator the ideal appliance for the job.

From a practical standpoint, you can use your dehydrator to turn items you might normally throw away into your own personal mix.

Homemade Potpourri

Items like fruit peels, nut shells, coconut shells, older flowers and apple or pear cores, which are normally discarded, become useful when you consider that they can add a bit of ambience to a room. When my wife uses cinnamon sticks in a recipe, I dehydrate them and toss them into the potpourri mix.

Makes 1 bowl

Apple or pear cores
Apple or pear peels
Citrus peels
Nut shells
Chopped coconut shells
Used cinnamon sticks
15 drops of your favorite essential oil
3 tablespoons (15 ml) water
Spray bottle

Spread the apple cores, apple peels, citrus peels, nut shells, coconut shells and cinnamon sticks over a covered surface. Add the essential oil drops and water to a small spray bottle, and lightly spray the ingredients to coat them.

Spread the items over dehydrator sheets, and dehydrate them at 120°F (49°C) for 8 to 10 hours, or until they are completely dried through.

Remove the dehydrated items, and give them a last light spritz from your spray bottle. Place them in a decorative bowl or a small paper bag. Set out as you'd like and enjoy the fragrance.

176   The Spicy Dehydrator Cookbook

Homemade Fire Starters

Remarkably, dried citrus peels make for excellent fire starters. Citrus peels contain oils that are concentrated when dehydrated, so be sure to put them to use. Dried citrus peels are superior to store-bought fire starters or paper for several reasons. They're cheaper, they produce less soot than paper and they smell great. Bonus!

Makes 1/2 cup (63 g)

Peels from 1 orange

Make sure your citrus peels are still fresh and show no signs of rotting. Wash them clean, and peel away the top layer, which contains the oils. Spread the peels over the dehydrator trays as evenly as possible. Dehydrate them at 135°F (57°C) until they are completely dried through. Light a couple of them up to get your fire started.

Store in airtight containers and use as needed.

Spent Grains

My wife and I have been craft beer lovers for many years. We enjoy beers of all types, as well as cooking, and this naturally led us to making our own beer. As with any learning process, it took a few times to get our batches to where we wanted them, but one thing we learned quickly is that you need a lot of grains to make beer. If you're making a typical 5-gallon (19-L) batch, you'll find yourself with several pounds of spent grains after your initial soaking.

The first question for me was, "What the heck can I do with this stuff?" I didn't want to throw the grains away. There was still a lot of life left in them. With a dehydrator, you can easily dry your spent grains, and then grind them into flour for use in all sorts of baked goods. It adds a nuttiness and depth of flavor you won't get anywhere else. Your friends will wonder what your secret ingredient is!

I've even heard of people making dog treats from the resulting flour. What a great idea!

If you're not a beer maker but are still curious about dehydrating spent grains at home, contact your local brewery. They are often more than willing to share their leftover grains with you. Normally they are donated to local farms for use as feed or simply thrown away. Why not feed yourself?

Spent Grain Flour

For most recipes, you can replace up to half of the required flour content with spent grain flour.

Makes 1 cup (120 g)

1 quart (950 ml) wet spent grains from brewing

Be sure your spent grains are drained as much as possible. They will still be moist. Spread them out over dehydrator sheets to ¼-inch (6-mm) thickness, or as close as you can. It can be difficult if you are dehydrating a lot at a time, though it will still dry if thicker.

Dehydrate at 125°F (52°C) for 10 to 12 hours, or until there is no detectable moisture left. Be sure to check with your fingers. If you notice any moisture spots, keep dehydrating until completely dried through.

Cool, and store in airtight containers. Grind up the grains in a food processor, spice grinder or, better yet, use a mill for finer powder. I find it's best to grind only what I need at the time.

Spent Grain Cookies

These are similar to oatmeal cookies in consistency, but the flavor is far more unique. You can add other ingredients, such as nuts or chocolate, to your personal tastes.

Makes 20 cookies

½ cup (60 g) Spent Grain Flour (page 179)

½ cup (60 g) all-purpose flour

½ teaspoon ground cinnamon

½ teaspoon baking soda

½ teaspoon salt

½ cup (120 g) softened butter

½ cup (90 g) brown sugar

¼ cup (50 g) granulated sugar

2 large eggs

1 teaspoon vanilla

1 cup (190 g) unprocessed dried spent grains

Raisins or chocolate chips, optional

Mix together the spent grain flour, all-purpose flour, cinnamon, baking soda and salt in a large bowl.

In a separate bowl, add the butter, brown sugar and granulated sugar. Use a hand mixer to cream the butter with the sugars for about 3 minutes. Add the eggs and vanilla, and mix until it is all combined.

Add the flour mixture to the sugar mixture, and stir it all together until a dough forms. Add the unprocessed dried spent grains and mix it together. It should be a bit chunky. Add the raisins or chocolate chips, if using.

Cover, and then refrigerate the dough for 30 minutes. This will make forming the cookies easier.

Heat the oven to 350°F (177°C). Hand roll the dough into about 20 small balls. Set them onto a lightly oiled baking sheet, and bake for 10 to 12 minutes, or until the edges crisp up and the centers are cooked through, yet soft. They will drop and spread, so leave room between them.

Transfer to a wire rack and cool.

Spent Grain Muffins

I like to make small muffins for a small, quick breakfast, though they are an excellent snack, too. These always disappear quickly.

Makes 30 small muffins

2 cups (240 g) Spent Grain Flour (page 179)

½ cup (100 g) granulated sugar

1 tablespoon (12 g) baking powder

½ teaspoon salt

1 cup (240 ml) milk

¼ cup (60 ml) vegetable oil

2 large eggs

1 teaspoon vanilla

Raisins, nuts or seeds, optional

Heat your oven to 425°F (218°C). Line a small muffin tin with papers.

Mix together that spent grain flour, sugar, baking powder and salt in a large bowl.

In a separate bowl, add the milk, oil, eggs and vanilla. Beat together until it is all combined. Pour into the dry ingredients and use a large fork to mix it together to form a batter. At this point you can add in raisins, nuts or seeds, if using.

Fill the muffin cups about three-quarters full, and bake for 15 to 20 minutes, or until they are cooked through. You can tell when they are done when a toothpick pulls out cleanly from the center.

Cool and enjoy. Muffins can be frozen and thawed for eating later.

Spent Grain Waffles

Make them sweet or savory. I enjoy mixing in chopped peppers, a nice Cajun seasoning blend or even a homemade beer cheese for a savory brunch.

Makes 6 to 8 waffles

1 cup (120 g) Spent Grain Flour (page 179)

1 cup (120 g) all-purpose flour

2 tablespoons (25 g) sugar

1 tablespoon (12 g) baking powder

½ teaspoon baking soda

½ teaspoon salt

1¾ cups (420 ml) milk

8 tablespoons (120 ml) melted butter

2 eggs

1 teaspoon vanilla

Sift together the spent grain flour, all-purpose flour, sugar, baking powder, baking soda and salt in a large bowl. In a separate bowl, whisk together the milk, butter, eggs and vanilla, and then slowly add them to the dry ingredients, stirring lightly until you have a lumpy batter.

Preheat the waffle iron and spray it with a bit of oil. Pour about ½ to ¾ cup (120 to 180 ml) of the batter into the waffle iron, per your iron's requirements, and cook according to the machine's instructions. It usually takes 2 to 3 minutes, depending on how dark and crispy you like your waffles.

These make some outstanding savory waffles if you add in other ingredients, like cheeses, peppers, seasoning blends and more.

Spent Grain Banana Bread

Banana bread has always been one of my favorite snacks, lightly toasted, with just a bit of butter slathered over a slice. Try this version with spent grains, which takes it to a whole new level.

Makes 1 loaf

½ cup (60 g) Spent Grain Flour (page 179)
1½ cups (180 g) all-purpose flour
1 teaspoon salt
1½ teaspoons (6 g) baking powder
¾ cup (160 g) sugar
8 tablespoons (240 g) butter, softened
2 eggs
3 ripe bananas, mashed
1 teaspoon vanilla extract
Raisins, nuts or chocolate chips, optional
Cream cheese frosting, optional

Heat your oven to 350°F (177°C). Lightly oil a 9 x 5 inch (23 x 13 cm) bread loaf pan.

Add the spent grain flour, all-purpose flour, salt, baking powder and sugar to a mixing bowl and sift them together.

Add the butter, eggs, bananas and vanilla extract to a food processor and process until nice and smooth. Stir the wet banana mixture into the dry ingredients just enough to combine them. At this point, gently fold the raisins, nuts or chocolate into the mix, if using.

Pour the batter into the bread loaf pan and bake for 50 minutes, or until the loaf is cooked through. You will know it is done when a toothpick comes out cleanly from the center.

Let the banana bread cool. You can enjoy it as-is like I do, or turn it into a dessert with a bit of cream cheese frosting.

Acknowledgments

A special THANKS to the whole crew at Page Street Publishing. I appreciate everything you've done to bring this book into the world. You have been outstanding to work with.

I would also like to thank everyone who has ever visited our website. You've all been great to hang with. You are the best people in the world!

A SUPER SHOUT OUT to all my family, friends and neighbors for listening to my incessant dehydration talk as I wrote this book, especially you, Natha! Our "Chef-mance" is now immortalized in writing.

Another shout out to Scorched Earth Brewing Company in Algonquin, Illinois. They helped me out when I needed spent grains for the "Practicals" chapter, and were happy to do it! I love sitting at your bar, and I always enjoy your quality craft beers.

AND! I would like to once again acknowledge my wife, Patty (though she's still also Crazy Patty and always will be), for everything she's done in my life and for this book. She is integral to all of my efforts, and without her, this book and our website at www.chilipeppermadness.com would only be a shadow of what they are.

She truly rocks.

About the Author

Mike Hultquist is the creator of Chili Pepper Madness, a food blog dedicated to creative yet approachable cooking with zesty food and big, bold flavors. His focus is on home cooking from scratch and bringing a bit of fun and spice to everyday meals.

Check out the site at www.chilipeppermadness.com.

Mike is also a fiction author and produced screenwriter. You can learn more about Mike's works at www.michaelhultquist.com.

A

alcohols, infused
- Apple Infused Bourbon, 172
- Bacon Infused Vodka, 171
- Tropical Infused Rum, 173

All-Purpose Veggie Seasoning, 14
Apple-Butternut Squash Soup, 104
Apple-Honeydew-Kiwi Fruit Leather, 38, *39*
Apple-Mango-Pear Fruit Leather, *36*, *37*
Apple Infused Bourbon, 172
Apple Pie Tea, 165

B

bacon recipes
- Bacon Infused Vodka, 171
- Creole Bacon Salt, 18
- Spicy Coffee-Maple Bacon Jerky, 92, *93*
- Sriracha-Honey Bacon Jerky, 74
- Sweet Barbecue Bacon Jerky, 76, *77*
- Thai Basil Bacon Jerky, 91

Banana Bread, Spent Grain, *184*, 185

beef recipes
- Chipotle-Bourbon Beef Jerky, 68, *69*
- Ghost Pepper Beef Jerky, *82*, 83
- Mongolian Beef Jerky, 75
- Sloppy Joes Jerky, 90
- Steakhouse Beef Jerky, 80, *81*

benefits of dehydrated foods, 8
Berry, Sweet Mixed, Rice Pudding, 150
Black Bean, Spicy, Soup, *106*, 107
Bourbon, Apple Infused, 172
Bread Crumbs, Herbed, 21
Buffalo Chicken Jerky, 87
Butternut Squash-Apple Soup, 104
Butternut Squash Risotto, *120*, 121

C

Cajun Rubbed Chicken Jerky, *78*, 79
Cajun, Ragin', Ghost Pepper Hot Sauce, 58, *59*

camping meals
- Butternut Squash Risotto, *120*, 121
- Chewy Power Bars, 136, *137*
- Chocolate-Strawberry Power Bars, 135
- Cinnamon-Banana Oatmeal, *132*, 133
- Coconut Chickpea Curry, *124*, 125
- how to make, 114
- Mexican-Style Couscous, 130, *131*
- Pasta Arrabbiata, *116*, 117
- Pasta Puttanesca, 118, *119*
- Pea and Sunflower Seed Risotto, *122*, *123*
- Red Beans and Rice, 126, *127*
- storing, 114
- Savory Red Bean Chili, *128*, 129
- Pineapple-Pear-Pecan Trail Mix, 134

Caribbean Style Aji Hot Sauce, 62, *63*
Carrot, Creamy, Soup, 112
Cauliflower, Spiced, Popcorn, *142*, 143
Cheesy Enchilada Soup, 113
Chewy Power Bars, 136, *137*

chicken recipes
- Buffalo Chicken Jerky, 87
- Cajun Rubbed Chicken Jerky, *78*, 79
- Chicken Fajita Jerky, 84, *85*
- Spicy Chicken Pozole, *100*, 101
- Sweet Habanero Chicken Jerky, 70, *71*

Chickpeas, Spiced, 148, *149*
Chili Pepper Madness blog, 6
Chili Powder, 23
Chili, Savory Red Bean, *128*, 129
Chinese-Style Chili Oil, 168
Chipotle-Bourbon Beef Jerky, 68, *69*
Chocolate-Banana Dessert, 154, *155*
Chocolate-Strawberry Power Bars, 135
Cinnamon-Banana Oatmeal, *132*, 133
Cinnamon-Mint Pears, *146*, 147
citrus peels, dried, as fire starters, 177
Citrus Pork Rub, 25
Citrus Salt, 16
Coconut Chickpea Curry, *124*, 125
Coconut Curry Soup, *110*, 111
Coconut-Rum Sugar, 20
Cookies, Spent Grain, 180, *181*
Creamy Carrot Soup, 112
Creole Bacon Salt, 18
Cuban Yuca Soup, 102, *103*

Cucumber-Lemon Water, 169
curry recipes
- Coconut Chickpea Curry, *124*, 125
- Coconut Curry Soup, *110, 111*

D

dehydrators
- basics, 9, 11
- sheets, for making leathers, 27–28
- types of, 6–7

dessert recipes
- Chocolate-Banana Dessert, 154, *155*
- Nectarine-Raspberry Dessert, 153

drinks and infusions. *See also* alcohols, infused
- Apple Pie Tea, 165
- Cucumber-Lemon Water, 169
- Ginger-Lemon Tea, 164

dryness of dehydrated foods, testing for, 11

F

Fire Starters, Homemade, 177
Flour, Spent Grain, *178*, 179
fruit leathers
- Apple-Honeydew-Kiwi Fruit Leather, 38, *39*
- Apple-Mango-Pear Fruit Leather, 36, *37*
- Cinnamon-Mint Pears, *146*, 147
- Ghost Pepper-Pineapple-Pear Hot Sauce Leather, 42, *43*
- Kiwi-Blueberry Leather, 46
- Mango-Habanero Hot Sauce Leather, 30, *31*
- Mango-Jalapeño-Pineapple Leather, 41
- Nutty Strawberry-Peach Energy Leather, *138*, 139
- Papaya-Pineapple-Grapefruit Fruit Leather, *32*, 33
- Salted Mint Watermelon Treats, 144, *145*
- Star Fruit-Kiwi-Pineapple Leather, 34, *35*
- Strawberry BBQ Sauce Leather, *49*, 50
- tips for making, 26
- Watermelon-Orange-Mango Fruit Leather, *44*, 45

Fruit Powder, 24

G

Garlic-Habanero Hot Sauce, *54, 55*
Ghost Pepper Beef Jerky, *82*, 83
Ghost Pepper-Pineapple-Pear Hot Sauce Leather, 42, *43*
Gazpacho, Winter, 105
Ginger-Lemon Tea, 164

H

Haitian Creole Hot Sauce, 57
Herbed Bread Crumbs, 21
Herbed Chili Oil, 168
hiking meals. *See* camping meals
Homemade Fire Starters, 177
Homemade Potpourri, 176
hot sauce leathers. *See also* salsa leathers
- Garlic-Habanero Hot Sauce, *54, 55*
- Ghost Pepper Beef Jerky, *82*, 83
- Ghost Pepper-Pineapple-Pear Hot Sauce Leather, 42, *43*
- Mango-Habanero Hot Sauce Leather, 30, *31*

hot sauces
- Caribbean Style Aji Hot Sauce, 62, *63*
- Garlic-Habanero Hot Sauce, *54, 55*
- Haitian Creole Hot Sauce, 57
- Mild Poblano Sauce, 64, *65*
- Quick Chili-Garlic Sauce, 56
- Ragin' Cajun Ghost Pepper Hot Sauce, 58, *59*
- storing, 53
- Superhot Hot Sauce, *60*, 61
- tips for making 52–53

I

infusions and teas
- Apple Pie Tea, 165
- Chinese-Style Chili Oil, 168
- Cucumber-Lemon Water, 169
- Ginger-Lemon Tea, 164
- Herbed Chili Oil, 168
- how to make, 162, 164
- Orange Chili Tea, 165
- Simple Chili Oil, 167

J

Jambalaya, *96*, 97
jerky recipes
- Buffalo Chicken Jerky, 87
- Cajun Rubbed Chicken Jerky, *78*, 79
- Chicken Fajita Jerky, 84, *85*
- Chipotle-Bourbon Beef Jerky, *68*, 69
- how to make, 66–67
- Mojo Pork Jerky, *72*, 73
- Mongolian Beef Jerky, 75
- Sesame Ginger Salmon Jerky, *88*, 89
- Sloppy Joes Jerky, 90
- Spicy Coffee-Maple Bacon Jerky, *92*, 93
- Sriracha-Honey Bacon Jerky, 74

Steakhouse Beef Jerky, 80, *81*
storing, 67
Sweet Barbecue Bacon Jerky, 76, *77*
Sweet Habanero Chicken Jerky, 70, *71*
Thai Basil Bacon Jerky, 91
Turkey Taco Jerky, 86

K

Kiwi-Blueberry Leather, 46

L

leathers
    Apple-Honeydew-Kiwi Fruit Leather, 38, *39*
    Apple-Mango-Pear Fruit Leather, 36, *37*
    Ghost Pepper-Pineapple-Pear Hot Sauce Leather, 42, *43*
    Kiwi-Blueberry Leather, 46
    Mango-Habanero Hot Sauce Leather, 30, *31*
    Mango-Jalapeño-Pineapple Leather, 41
    Nutty Strawberry-Peach Energy Leather, *137*, 138
    Papaya-Pineapple-Grapefruit Fruit Leather, 32, *33*
    Salsa Verde Leather, 47
    Spicy Red Salsa Leather, 48, *49*
    Sriracha Leather, *28*, 29
    Star Fruit-Kiwi-Pineapple Leather, 34, *35*
    storing, 27
    Strawberry BBQ Sauce Leather, *49*, 50
    tips for making, 26
    Watermelon-Orange-Mango Fruit Leather, 44, *45*
lemon juice, in dehydrating, 11

M

Mango-Habanero Hot Sauce Leather, 30, *31*
Mango-Jalapeño-Pineapple Leather, 41
meals, easy dehydrated
    Butternut Squash Risotto, *120*, 121
    Cinnamon-Banana Oatmeal, *132*, 133
    Coconut Chickpea Curry, *124*, 125
    how to make, 114
    Mexican-Style Couscous, 130, *131*
    Pasta Arrabbiata, *116*, 117
    Pasta Puttanesca, 118, *119*
    Pea and Sunflower Seed Risotto, 122, *123*
    Red Beans and Rice, 126, *127*
    storing, 114
    Savory Red Bean Chili, *128*, 129
Mexican recipes
    Caldo de Cameron (Mexican Shrimp Soup), 98, *99*
    Cheesy Enchilada Soup, 113
    Mexican-Style Couscous, 130, *131*
    Mild Poblano Sauce, *64*, 65
    Salsa Verde Leather, 47
    Spicy Black Bean Soup, *106*, 107
    Spicy Chicken Pozole, *100*, 101
    Spicy Red Salsa Leather, 48, *49*
Mojo Pork Jerky, *72*, 73
Mongolian Beef Jerky, 75
Muffins, Spent Grain, 182
Mushroom and Quinoa Soup, 108, *109*

N

Nectarine-Raspberry Dessert, 153
Nutty Strawberry-Peach Energy Leather, *138*, 139

O

Oatmeal, Cinnamon-Banana, *132*, 133
oil infusions
    Chinese-Style Chili Oil, 168
    Herbed Chili Oil, 168
    Simple Chili Oil, 167
Orange Chili Tea, 165

P

Papaya-Pineapple-Grapefruit Fruit Leather, *32*, 33
Pasta Arrabbiata, *116*, 117
Pasta Puttanesca, 118, *119*
Pea and Sunflower Seed Risotto, 122, *123*
Pineapple-Pear-Pecan Trail Mix, 134
Pineapple-Mango Dessert, 151
Poblano Sauce, Mild, *64*, 65
pork recipes
    Mojo Pork Jerky, *72*, 73
    Sriracha-Honey Bacon Jerky, 74
    Sweet Barbecue Bacon Jerky, 76, *77*
Potato Matchsticks, Zesty, 158, *159*
Potpourri, Homemade, 176

Q

Quick Chili-Garlic Sauce, 56
Quinoa, Mushroom and, Soup, 108, *109*

R

Ragin' Cajun Ghost Pepper Hot Sauce, 58, *59*
Red Beans and Rice, 126, *127*

rice recipes
    Butternut Squash Risotto, *120*, 121
    Jambalaya, *96*, 97
    Pea and Sunflower Seed Risotto, 122, *123*
    Red Beans and Rice, 126, *127*
    Sweet Mixed Berry Rice Pudding, 150
Roasted Garlic-Chili Salt, 17
Rum, Tropical Infused, 173

S

Salmon, Sesame Ginger, Jerky, *88*, 89
salsa leathers
    Salsa Verde Leather, 47
    Spicy Red Salsa Leather, 48, *49*
Salted Mint Watermelon Treats, 144, *145*
salts
    Citrus Salt, 16
    Creole Bacon Salt, 18
    Roasted Garlic-Chili Salt, 17
sauces, tomato
    arrabbiata, *116*, 117
    puttanesca, 118, *119*
Savory Red Bean Chili, *128*, 129
seasoning blends and powders
    All-Purpose Veggie Seasoning, 14
    Chili Powder, 23
    Citrus Pork Rub, 25
    Citrus Salt, 16
    Coconut-Rum Sugar, 20
    Creole Bacon Salt, 18
    Fruit Powder, 24
    Herbed Bread Crumbs, 21
    Roasted Garlic-Chili Salt, 17
    Shrimp Powder, 22
    Tequila-Lime Sugar, 19
    Veggie Stock Powder, 15
Sesame Ginger Salmon Jerky, *88*, 89
shrimp recipes
    Caldo de Cameron (Mexican Shrimp Soup), 98, *99*
    Jambalaya, *96*, 97
    Shrimp Powder, 22
Simple Chili Oil, 167
Sloppy Joes Jerky, 90
snacks and munchies
    Chocolate-Banana Dessert, 154, *155*
    Nectarine-Raspberry Dessert, 153
    Pineapple-Mango Dessert, 151
    Salted Mint Watermelon Treats, 144, *145*
    Spiced Cauliflower Popcorn, *142*, 143
    Spiced Chickpeas, 148, *149*
    Sweet and Spicy Sweet Potato Chips, *160*, 161
    Sweet Mixed Berry Rice Pudding, 150
    Wicked Veggie Chips, *156*, 157
    Zesty Potato Matchsticks, 158, *159*
soup recipes
    Apple-Butternut Squash Soup, 104
    Caldo de Cameron (Mexican Shrimp Soup), 98, *99*
    Coconut Curry Soup, *110*, 111
    Creamy Carrot Soup, 112
    Cuban Yuca Soup, 102, *103*
    Jambalaya, *96*, 97
    Mushroom and Quinoa Soup, 108, *109*
    Spicy Black Bean Soup, *106*, 107
    Spicy Chicken Pozole, *100*, 101
    Veggie Stock Powder, 15
    Winter Gazpacho, 105
spent grain recipes
    Spent Grain Banana Bread, *184*, 185
    Spent Grain Cookies, 180, *181*
    Spent Grain Flour, *178*, 179
    Spent Grain Muffins, 182
    Spent Grain Waffles, 183
Spiced Cauliflower Popcorn, *142*, 143
Spiced Chickpeas, 148, *149*
Spicy Black Bean Soup, *106*, 107
Spicy Chicken Pozole, *100*, 101
Sriracha Leather, *28*, 29
stew recipes. *See* soup recipes
Strawberry-Peach, Nutty, Energy Leather, *138*, 139
Sweet and Spicy Sweet Potato Chips, *160*, 161
Sweet Barbecue Bacon Jerky, 76, *77*
Sweet Mixed Berry Rice Pudding, 150

T

tea blends
    Apple Pie Tea, 165
    making, 164
    Ginger-Lemon Tea, 164
    Orange Chili Tea, 165
Tequila-Lime Sugar, 19
Thai Basil Bacon Jerky, 91
Trail Mix, Pineapple-Pear-Pecan, 134
Tropical Fruit Infused Rum, 173
Turkey Taco Jerky, 86

V

vegetarian recipes
    Butternut Squash Risotto, *120*, 121

Coconut Chickpea Curry, *124,* 125
Veggie Chips, Wicked, *156, 157*
veggie seasoning, 14
Veggie Stock Powder, 15

W
Waffles, Spent Grain, 183
Water, Cucumber-Lemon, 169
Watermelon-Orange-Mango Fruit Leather, *44, 45*
Watermelon, Salted Mint, Treats, 144, *145*
Wicked Veggie Chips, *156, 157*
Winter Gazpacho, 105

Z
Zesty Potato Matchsticks, 158, *159*

As a member of 1% for the Planet, Page Street Publishing protects our planet by donating to nonprofits like The Trustees, which focuses on local land conservation. Learn more at onepercentfortheplanet.org.